Believe In Miracles But Trust In Jesus

BELIEVE IN MIRACLES BUT TRUST IN JESUS

ADRIAN ROGERS

CROSSWAY BOOKS • WHEATON, ILLINOIS
A DIVISION OF GOOD NEWS PUBLISHERS

Believe in Miracles But Trust in Jesus

Published by Crossway Books
a division of Good News Publishers
1300 Crescent Street
Wheaton, Illinois 60187

Cover design: Cindy Kiple

Cover illustration: Pixel Graphics

First printing, 1997

First trade paperback edition, 1999

Printed in the United States of America

Unless otherwise indicated, bible quotations are taken from the King James Version.

Library of Congress Cataloging-in-Publication Data

Rogers, Adrian.
Believe in miracles but trust in Jesus / Adrian Rogers.
p. cm.
Includes bibliographical references.
ISBN 1-58134-076-1
1. Miracles. 2. Christian life—Baptist authors. 3. Jesus Christ—Miracles. 4. Bible N.T. Gospel John—Criticism., interpretation, etc. I. Title.
BT97.2.R32 1997
226.7'06—dc21 96-29651

15 14 13 12 11 10 09 08 07 06 05 04 03 02 01 00 · 99
15 14 13 12 11 10 9 8 7 6 5 4 3 2

This book is dedicated to the congregation and staff of Bellevue Baptist Church in Memphis, Tennessee.

No pastor could ever have a more loving and caring congregation. Mine is the wonderful privilege and awesome responsibility to pastor this church.

Thank you, people of Bellevue, and dear, dear staff, for your "work of faith, and labor of love, and patience of hope in our Lord Jesus Christ, in the sight of God and our Father."

Devotedly,
Adrian Rogers

CONTENTS

ACKNOWLEDGMENTS

Once again, I want to thank the people whose support and encouragement helped to make this book possible: the staff at Love Worth Finding Ministries; Linda Glance, my faithful secretary who spent many hours typing portions of this manuscript; President Lane Dennis, Vice President Len Goss, Managing Editor Ted Griffin, and all the helpful people at Crossway Books; and my editor and friend, Philip Rawley.

INTRODUCTION

Between 1925 and 1963 one could drive the highways of America and read delightful red and white signs that dotted those roads. They were advertisements for a shaving cream known as Burma-Shave.

If you are middle-aged, you may remember these. There would be a succession of small signs, maybe one foot by two feet, set in the ground on sticks. They would be placed one after another in intervals of about a quarter-mile or so.

You would have to read each sign as you rode along before you would get to the punch line. The entire thing often took the form of a little poem. For example:

A peach looks good
With lots of fuzz.
But a man is no peach
And never wuz.

You would ride a bit further, and the last sign would say, "Burma-Shave!" You got a portion of the message with each sign, but it all came together at the end.

That is an understandable example of what the apostle John was doing when he wrote his Gospel. The beloved apostle selected for us seven miracles that bring as much encouragement to us who live in the twentieth century as they did to those who experienced them in the first century. They are life-changing!

A Parade of Miracles

At the end of John's Gospel we learn that there was a selection process going on as far as his recording of Christ's miracles was concerned. By the inspiration of the Holy Spirit, John chose seven of the Lord's miracles and put them together in a special sequence for our understanding:

> *And many other signs truly did Jesus in the presence of his disciples, which are not written in this book: but these are written, that ye might believe that Jesus is the Christ, the Son of God; and that believing ye might have life through his name.*
>
> —*John 20:30-31*

The word "signs" in this passage has great significance. It is the plural of the Greek word *semeion,* which means a "miracle with a message" or a "miracle with a meaning." Not just a miracle at face value, but a miracle with a special lesson tied to it. It is a sign with special significance.

Dr. G. Campbell Morgan said that every parable Jesus spoke was a miracle of instruction and every miracle Jesus performed was a parable for instruction. I like that. There is meaning in these miracles John records.

Each of these seven miracles of Jesus shows not only His power over nature, but His redeeming power over sin, death, hell, and the grave.

These miracles point clearly to the wonderful truth that Jesus Christ is God's answer to our deepest needs. He is God's answer to your disappointments, doubts, disabilities, desires, despair, darkness, and death.

In this study we are going to learn to believe in miracles, but to trust in Jesus. We are going to learn that miracles of grace are greater than miracles of glory.

This book will affirm your faith in the supernatural. My prayer for you is that you will experience miracles in your life. But I would be disappointed if that is as far as you get. *We need to go beyond miracles and go on to Jesus*. When we receive Him and truly know His transforming power, we have experienced the ultimate miracle.

As the song says:

It took a miracle to put the stars in place,
It took a miracle to hang the world in space;
But when He saved my soul,
Cleansed and made me whole,
It took a miracle of love and grace!

Bill Gaither once wrote a song that included these words: "There is a long parade of miracles, and it is led by a wonderful King." Indeed, that is so, and I am one of those miracles. Are you?

CHAPTER ONE

THE POSSIBILITY OF MIRACLES

* * *

I have good news for you. There is nothing wrong with you that a miracle would not cure. All you need is a miracle.

And I believe in miracles. I really do! Those who have problems with the possibility of miracles really have difficulty with the fact that there is a sovereign God. If one can accept Genesis 1:1 in the Bible, he should have little difficulty believing in the possibility of the miraculous.

God spoke, and the universe sprang into existence. Billions of galaxies spread across the black velvet of space. Planet Earth swung into space and began to teem with life.

It is unthinkable that the Creator, having such incredible power, should subsequently be unable to move miraculously upon His own creation. Is the clock stronger than the clockmaker? No indeed! God is not a helpless onlooker to the work of His hands. The psalmist declares, "The heavens are thine, the earth also is thine: as for the world and the fulness thereof, thou hast founded them" (Psalm 89:11).

Dr. Robert G. Lee, a great preacher now in heaven, has rightly said, "God is not a bewildered bellhop running up and down the corridors of the hotel He created trying to find the right key."

God is not bounded by the laws of nature because there really are no laws of nature. What men call the laws of nature are in truth the laws of God that nature must obey.

Years ago I heard a delightful story. Dr. Lee Scarbrough, one of the early presidents of Southwestern Baptist Theological Seminary and a great preacher of the Word, was preaching about Jonah being swallowed by a great fish.

Later at home, Dr. Scarbrough's little son asked a straightforward question. "Daddy, do you really believe that a fish could swallow a man and keep the man alive inside for three days and three nights?"

The wise father replied, "Son, if God could make a man out of absolutely nothing to begin with, and if God could create the first sea creatures from absolutely nothing, don't you think He would have the power to make a fish that could swallow a man and keep him alive for three days and nights if He wanted to?"

The little fellow replied, "Well, if you're going to bring God into it, that's different."

Amen! That's what I believe. I believe in miracles because I believe in God. I would remind all of us of the angel's question to Abraham: "Is any thing too hard for the LORD?" (Genesis 18:14).

I hear someone reply, "Well, I don't believe in God. Therefore, I don't believe in miracles."

But whoever says that must believe that nothing times nobody equals everything. The doubter must believe that in the beginning the heavens and the earth created themselves and then generated life spontaneously. Such a person believes in a colossal miracle without anyone to perform it.

Anyone who adopts this as his belief should not pride himself on his intelligence. The greatest minds of all time have believed in a Creator. Socrates, Lord Bacon, Galileo, John Newton, Louis Pasteur, Albert Einstein, and Wernher von Braun all believed in a higher intelligence.

It is impossible to believe in a sovereign God and not believe in miracles. Ignorance of God makes belief impossible, but knowledge of Him makes unbelief impossible. "Why should it be thought a thing incredible with you, that God should raise the dead?" Paul asked Agrippa (Acts 26:8).

What do we mean when we use the word *supernatural* to describe God and His works? *Supernatural* merely means "above nature." God is sovereign over nature. The law of gravity is overruled when a magnet picks up iron filings. The superior law of magnetism has taken over. In like fashion, the superior law of divine sovereignty overrules the lesser laws of nature. The patriarch Job said of God:

> *He looketh to the ends of the earth, and seeth under the whole heaven; to make the weight for the winds; and he weigheth the waters by measure. When he made a decree for the rain, and a way for the lightning of the thunder; then did he see it, and declare it; he prepared it, yea, and searched it out.*
>
> —*Job 28:24-27*

We don't have to prove miracles. Christians really don't need proof, and an unbelieving world wouldn't accept it. We need not be afraid of science. Christians should enjoy and appreciate science even more than unbelievers.

If a scientist has a good word to say about God and miracles, that should give us no more faith in miracles, but a little more confidence in the scientist. We do not need to defend or explain miracles. Let's just enjoy them.

PRESENT-DAY MIRACLES

Beyond the clear statements of the biblical text, one would have to admit that miracles happen in present-day life.

God still supernaturally heals the sick. Such a statement prompts raised eyebrows among many more reserved believers. These people have seen the excesses, manipulations, and frauds of the modern-day, so-called divine healing movement. They are so afraid of wildfire that they have settled for no fire.

I have wondered what would happen in some of our cut-and-dried prayer meetings if God were to answer from heaven with a bona fide, industrial-strength miracle of healing right there on the spot. In some churches, it is all right to pray for healing just so long as nobody gets healed.

Let me pause here to say that I, too, am aware of the charlatans and hucksters who parade up and down the land claiming to heal the sick. I will pay my respects to them later in this volume.

But having said that, I must say that I believe God does heal today—sovereignly, supernaturally, radically, and dramatically. In fact, I want to tell you about a precious friend I have known for twenty years. Her name is Marolyn Ford, and her story is an incredible testimony to the healing power of God.

As a young lady, Marolyn began to lose her eyesight. It progressively got worse and worse. The doctor told her she had an irreversible problem called macular deterioration. He predicted that it would progress until she would be legally blind. This indeed happened. She lost her sight and had to go to a school for the blind and learn to tap with a cane and read Braille.

But the story does not end there. She went away to a Bible college to study. The professors allowed her to take classes with a tape recorder. There, as a sightless young girl, she met a young ministerial student named Acie Ford. They fell in love, and this young preacher married a bride who was beautiful but could not see her bridegroom.

God gave them a little baby. She could not see the face of her baby either. God gave them a wonderful church, and she knew her church members by voice but could not see their faces.

Marolyn had prayed many times that she might be healed by miracle or medicine, but nothing seemed to help. One evening after a time of ministry, she and her husband were driving home late at night. They discussed Marolyn's blindness. Acie talked to her about the impediment it was to the ministry and how wonderful it would be if God would heal her. Let Marolyn tell you what happened in her own words, taken from her book *These Blind Eyes Now See*:

That evening both of us were exhausted. Acie picked up a religious periodical, and I climbed into bed. After reading a minute, Acie put the magazine down, got on his knees for our nightly devotion, and began praying.

We both began to cry as he prayed with great feeling and boldness: "Oh, God! You can restore Marolyn's eyesight tonight, Lord. I know You can do it! And, God, if it be Your will, I pray You will do it tonight." Perhaps neither of us was quite prepared for what happened. After 12 blurred and dark years, there was sharpness and light.

"Acie, I can see!" I exclaimed.

"You're kidding," he answered.

I repeated, "I can see! I can see the pupils in your eyes!"

Acie thought that perhaps just a little vision had come back.

I said, "Acie, it's 12:30 at night! You need a shave! I can see!"

Acie still couldn't believe the miracle that had really occurred. He grabbed a newspaper, pointed to the large print at the top of the page, and asked, "Can you see this?" "I can do better than that!" I exclaimed. "I can read the smaller print!"

Acie got excited. "Marolyn, can you see the dresser? Can you see the bed?"

We shouted and praised the Lord for what He had done! Such a miracle was overwhelming. Things had been rough for Acie lately as he tried to keep up with both his church work and his sales job. He had nearly reached his limit that evening when the miracle happened. We knew that God was able, but we couldn't comprehend that something so wonderful and miraculous had happened to us.

Jumping off the bed, Acie asked the question again, "Marolyn, you can see?"

"Yes!"

"Praise God! Praise God! Praise God! Glory, glory, glory to God! It can't be!" Acie exclaimed.

We were beside ourselves with happiness. "This is heaven!" Acie shouted. "It has to be! Oh, God, why did I doubt You?"

Then he turned to me. "Why did I doubt God? I didn't believe He could do something like this! He did it!"

Psalm 116:12—"What shall I render unto the LORD for all his benefits toward me?"—came to Acie's mind. We were jumping up and down and crying at the same time. I was getting my first look at my husband. For the first time, I could see his face, his eyes, his nose, his mouth. I could see!

I ran to look in the mirror. I could hardly believe how my facial features had changed. I had become blind at 19; now I was 31. I kept taking a second look. . . .

We reached for the phone to call our parents. When the phone rang at my parents' home in Michigan, Mother was awake—she had not been able to sleep that night. For years she had been burdened with the thought of my blindness and her own helplessness in not being able to do anything about it. How happy our news made her! She rejoiced with us over the telephone lines. I asked her to share the news with the others in my family who lived in Holland, Michigan, and with my twin sister in New York.

Acie dialed his parents, and his mother sleepily answered. Acie shouted, "Mother, Marolyn can see!"

Mom Ford had been awakened in the middle of the night by a son too excited to speak calmly. She asked, "Is everything all right?" But Acie could only repeat over and over: "Marolyn can see! Marolyn can see! She can see!"

We tried to explain to Mom and Dad Ford, but we had so little time. There were many other phone calls to make. We wanted to run down the street at 1 A.M. and shout that I was blind, but now I see![1]

The director for the school for the blind said she should go to the doctor and let him confirm this miracle.

The doctor who had examined her before in her blindness put the eye charts in front of her. She read them with ease. He said to her, "I cannot doubt or deny that you can see. Now let me look into your eyes."

When he did, he gave a gasp. He said, "I don't understand it. There is really no change. A portion of your eyes are like a mirror that had the quicksilver scraped off." He said it was a bigger miracle than he would have believed. "It is impossible for you to see and yet you see."

In the years since then, Marolyn has crossed America giving her testimony. It has blessed and strengthened thousands. She does not believe it is always God's will to heal, but she cannot deny what God has done for her.

I am blessed constantly when I am around this humble and dedicated couple who have seen God do a miracle. To look into Marolyn's beautiful blue eyes gives one the feeling that he is seeing with his own eyes an undeniable, supernatural work of God.

Another incident of God's sovereign power comes to mind. We were in Moscow, Russia, during the Orthodox Easter. An elaborate sound stage had been constructed in Red Square by Campus Crusade for Christ. There was to be a concert and then a Gospel presentation. Many thousands had gathered, and the service was to be telecast throughout all Russia.

I was with Dr. Bill Bright, the founder of Campus Crusade, in prayer when a messenger came with the news, "It's raining. Because power lines are down everywhere, the government officials say that we must shut down the event."

"We can't do that. Too much money, time, and faith have been invested," Bill Bright said. The leadership of our event pleaded with the officials for just ten more minutes to give the rain time to stop. It looked impossible. Gray clouds covered the sky over the Kremlin. The cold rain fell on our heads.

A group of prayer warriors huddled under a scaffold and began to sing and pray. I can hear them now and see them in my memory as they looked up into the face of those threatening clouds and called out, "Stop the rain, Lord, stop the rain."

I testify to you that in nine and a half minutes an amazing thing happened. It seemed as if a giant squeegee were drawn across the sky. A blazing sun began to smile from an azure sky. Our God had answered prayer. The program that followed had another touch of His mighty power.

We rejoice in these kinds of stories. We must admit that God heals by miracle, and also by medicine and other natural means as it seems wise to Him. Sometimes He heals instantaneously, sometimes over long periods of time. And if we are twice born, we know that He always heals in eternity.

MIRACLES OF PROVIDENCE

Not only are there miracles of healing and wonders in nature, there are miracles of God's providential guidance.

I personally have experienced what I would call miraculous

answers to prayer. Some of our prayer answers might be dismissed as mere coincidence, but indeed some cannot.

In one such instance, I had lost my billfold—where and how I knew not. A lost billfold is aggravating, to say the least. Over and over I mentally and physically retraced my steps.

Then I began to think the normal troubling thoughts for such a time: "I'll have to get another driver's license. I'll have to cancel the credit cards. And what about the other important papers?"

But then I got convicted in my spirit. "Lord, I have been more concerned about a lost billfold than about lost souls. Forgive me. I will worry no more. I commit it to you." That's how I prayed that afternoon.

Here is the strange part. That night while my head was on the pillow, just before I drifted off to sleep, I prayed, "Lord, show me in a dream where my billfold is."

I say this was strange because I had never before asked God to show me anything in a dream. I generally try to keep a little distance from people who want to tell me about their dreams, if you know what I mean.

Yet that was my prayer. And dream I did. I saw in my dream my billfold. It was lying in a big blue mail box—the kind that sits on the corner so people can deposit letters in it.

In my dream I had X-ray vision. I could see right through the box and right into the billfold. I could see cards and even an old Roman coin someone had given me still in the billfold. I also saw that the few dollars that had been in it were no longer there.

The next morning my secretary said, "Pastor, you have a call from the postmaster."

"Mr. Rogers?"

"Yes."

"We have your billfold."

"Don't tell me—I'll tell you," I replied. Then I described to the postmaster the big blue mailbox. I told him that my billfold was in the mailbox, and I described the contents that remained in it.

He was amazed. Maybe he thought I'd put it in there, I don't know, but actually I had seen it in my dream.

To this day, I've not been able to understand all that was involved in that episode. Perhaps God was saying to me, "You were right just to trust Me about the billfold. I knew where it was the whole time."

The one thing I do know is that this answer to prayer made an incredible impact on me. There was no way this could have been coincidence. This special revelation, as far as I was concerned, was in the realm of the miraculous.

I am not an expert in dreams, so don't come to me with yours. All I am saying is that God does do miraculous things. We all have to admit it. I firmly believe in miracles.

MIRACLES AND THE INTELLECT

You don't have to check your brain at the door to believe in miracles.

On April 9, 1996, Supreme Court Justice Antonin Scalia delivered an address at the invitation of the Mississippi College School of Law. The address that this brilliant Supreme Court judge gave generated a firestorm of criticism among the indignant members of the liberal press.

The sixty-year-old Roman Catholic gave a scathing portrayal of a society that disparages religious belief and especially the beliefs of Christians. Justice Scalia used both sarcasm and humor, for which he is well-known.

He facetiously declared that "the worldly wise do not believe in the resurrection of the dead. It is really quite absurd [to them]." He continued in the same vein saying, "So everything from the Easter morning to the Ascension has to be made up by the groveling enthusiasts as part of their plan to get themselves martyred. . . . The wise do not investigate such silliness," he said sarcastically. They "do not believe."

"A general belief in God is one thing," Scalia said, but it is "quite another matter to embrace the miracles of the Virgin Birth of Christ, His rising from the dead, and His own ascension from the grave. Yet, it is 'irrational' to reject miracles a priori," he argued, echoing G. K. Chesterton and St. Thomas Aquinas. "One can be sophisticated and believe in God. Reason and intellect are not to be laid aside where matters of religion are concerned. What is irrational [is] to reject . . . the possibility of miracles and the resurrection of Jesus Christ, which is precisely what the worldly wise do."

In summing up this masterful address, Judge Scalia declared, "We must pray for the courage to endure the scorn of the sophisticated world. . . . We are fools for Christ's sake."[2] The audience of more than 650 persons stood to their feet and gave this courageous man a standing ovation.

Are miracles possible? We must say a resounding yes to that. Can we have miracles on demand? That's another question.

But I can promise you this—God wants to do a great and wonderful miracle just for you. This is what the Gospel of John is all about. John wrote to show us that *the miracles of grace are greater than the miracles of glory*.

The greatest miracle is the transformation that God works when He regenerates a soul. That is not a dodge on my part. That is not some slippery escape clause. That is absolute truth, and that is why John wrote his Gospel.

> *And many other signs truly did Jesus in the presence of his disciples, which are not written in this book: but these are written, that ye might believe that Jesus is the Christ, the Son of God; and that believing ye might have life through his name.*
>
> *—John 20:30-31*

CHAPTER TWO

THE PROBLEMS WITH MIRACLES

* * *

When it comes to miracles, all is not sweetness and light. To get a proper perspective on the miraculous, we must face some very difficult and perplexing problems.

THE PROBLEM OF DECEPTION

The Bible prophesies that a coming world ruler will be energized by Satan. He is called the Antichrist, the beast, the man of sin, the son of perdition. He will be Satan incarnate.

This wicked impostor will have a sinister minister of propaganda who will go before him. That forerunner is called the false prophet, and he will have a dark and devilish power to work miracles:

> *And I beheld another beast coming up out of the earth; and he had two horns like a lamb, and he spake as a dragon. And he exerciseth*

> *all the power of the first beast before him, and causeth the earth and them which dwell therein to worship the first beast, whose deadly wound was healed. And he doeth great wonders, so that he maketh fire come down from heaven on the earth in the sight of men, and deceiveth them that dwell on the earth by the means of those miracles which he had power to do in the sight of the beast; saying to them that dwell on the earth, that they should make an image to the beast, which had the wound by a sword, and did live.*
>
> *—Revelation 13:11-14*

It is obvious that in the future a worldwide deception will come riding upon the wings of the miraculous. When Antichrist arrives, the world will be steeped in New-Age mysticism and will be easy plucking for this master magician with his bag full of tricks.

This is why *true faith must go beyond miracles and go on to Jesus.* Let me illustrate.

Suppose you wanted the assurance of salvation and you prayed, "Lord, speak to me. Give me a sign."

Then suppose an angel, bright, shiny, and glorious, were to appear and say, "My child, God has sent me to give you this message of comfort. He is well pleased with you."

You ask, "Please, mighty angel, I must be sure. Can you give me more assurance?"

"Yes," he answers. "Behold!" At that moment the heavens blaze from pole to pole with a fiery glory.

"Oh, thank you, mighty angel," you reply in ecstasy. "I will never doubt again."

Then comes the end and the final judgment. The Book of Life is opened, and your name is not there.

"But, Lord," you say, "I saw an angel, and he came to me and gave me such glorious assurance."

Satan could say at that moment, "You fool! That was me, transformed as an angel of light." What does the Scripture say? "And no marvel; for Satan himself is transformed into an angel of light" (2 Corinthians 11:14).

You continue to protest. "What about the fiery display of glory?"

Satan again could say, "Indeed, you are a fool. I was the one who deceived you with that fire from heaven." Did we not just read in Revelation 13:13 that the false prophet "doeth great wonders, so that he maketh fire come down from heaven on the earth in the sight of men?"

What one sees is not always what one gets.

One day my wife, Joyce, and I were waiting in London's Gatwick Airport for our flight to depart. Joyce was shopping for a teapot, and I was trying to entertain myself in some way. I had a few extra pounds (the kind you can spend), and I spotted a theater featuring a virtual reality experience. I sat in a computerized and motorized seat as a show began on the screen.

This particular experience was a motorcycle ride. On the screen the scenery screamed past. The motorcycle rumbled and roared. The seat I was on leaned, bucked, jumped, and vibrated. My heart began to pound. I held on tight! Talk about Mr. Toad's Wild Ride at Disney World! Moments later I walked away from there and back into the airport. I had in reality only been sitting in a chair. Yet to this moment I remember that "ride."

Antichrist will be able to make people believe his lies with more than modern technology. He will have devilish power. It will be virtual reality but not *virtuous* reality—the power of one "whose coming is after the working of Satan with all power and signs and lying wonders" (2 Thessalonians 2:9).

Does Satan indeed have this kind of power? You'd better believe it! With his counterfeit credentials and deceptive power, he would "deceive the very elect" if it were possible (Matthew 24:24). He is the master of magic and disguise. This minister of destruction is not always ugly. He is sometimes hideously beautiful and comes as an angel of light.

Let me again affirm that I believe God works miracles. But they confirm the Word of God; they do not supersede it. If the unpardonable sin is to attribute to the Devil the work of the Holy Spirit, would it not be equally dangerous to attribute to the Holy Spirit the work of the Devil?

We believe in a mighty God for whom nothing is impossible. But always remember that the extraordinary is primarily meant to support the exposition of the Word of God. The Word made clear redeems a soul. It sets forth salvation's plan. Signs and miracles in themselves cannot do this.

When the Holy Spirit came upon some in the early church, God confirmed the Word with wonders. Simon the magician saw these. He had been mystifying the people of Samaria with demonic powers. He wanted to get in on what the apostles were doing. So he offered Peter money.

"Thy money perish with thee," Peter shouted to this charlatan (Acts 8:20). Then Peter continued to speak "the word of the Lord" (Acts 8:25)—that is, he preached the Gospel in order to bring people to salvation.

A MIRACLE A DAY?

Someone coined this little gem: "A miracle a day keeps the Devil away." Oh? It could be that he is the one doing the miracles!

Miracles, even those done by Almighty God, don't seem to be a great help in building up believers. When Jesus turned water into wine, the crowds began to surge behind Him. He had the status of a celebrity. But that was not what His heart longed for. Jesus could read the motives of these miracle-mongers:

> *Now when he was in Jerusalem at the passover, in the feast day, many believed in his name, when they saw the miracles which he did. But Jesus did not commit himself unto them, because he knew all men, and needed not that any should testify of man; for he knew what was in man.*
>
> —*John 2:23-25*

This same crowd of "believers" would leave Him like rats deserting a sinking ship when He began to call for real surrender and personal communion with Himself. He had to turn to His own disciples and ask, "Will ye also go away?" (John 6:67).

MIRACLES WERE NOT PUBLIC RELATIONS

Jesus did miracles, and He still does them, but not as publicity stunts. He did not need nor want the fellowship that comes only on the basis of miracles. To the contrary, He would sometimes ask the disciples or those He healed not to tell anyone about the miracle He had just performed.

Perhaps another illustration will help. Imagine a man who is rich and powerful. Yet he is old and will soon leave his legacy of millions to someone. He has only two potential heirs, a niece and a nephew.

The niece and nephew often have their rich uncle over to their houses for dinner. They fawn over him, cook for him, and seem to enjoy the funny stories he tells.

Now here is the uncle's problem. Do his young relatives really enjoy being around an old man like him? Would he get a pillow for his back and a second piece of homemade pie if he were as poor as the niece and nephew? Do they love him for who he is, or for what he has and for what his money can do?

This man wants to be loved for who he is. If the love is real, he will have little problem sharing what he has.

Likewise, God wants us to love Him for who He is. That's why when Jesus came into the world, He laid aside all of the glory and splendor that belonged to Him in heaven. He laid aside the outward manifestations of deity, but kept all the beauty of His holy nature and the character that was His as God.

Why did He not come into this world in a jeweled chariot, wearing regal robes? Why was He born in a stable with cow dung on the floor? Why was He born to a peasant mother? Why was He reared in an obscure village in the home of a lowly carpenter?

Why did Isaiah say of Him, "For he shall grow up before him as a tender plant, and as a root out of a dry ground: he hath no form nor comeliness; and when we shall see him, there is no beauty that we should desire him" (53:2)?

The reason is that Jesus wanted His followers to love Him for who He was, not for what He had or what He could do.

If God wanted to, He could overwhelm us, bribe us, or coerce us with a dazzling display of glory and omnipotence. Even the most wicked would tremble and fall on their faces at this display, but this is not what God wants.

Real faith is not a matter of being overwhelmed by what the eyes see, but by what the heart feels in His presence.

Faith is the heart's response to the character and nature of Jesus apart from His outward miracle-working power. When the eye is right, it responds to light; when the ear is right, it responds to sound; and when the heart is right, it responds to Jesus. That response is called faith.

May I make a confession? As a young boy I went into a room, got down on my knees, and asked God to do a miracle. I said, "Lord, I want You to move this chair from one side of the room to the other."

Now don't laugh at me, please. I was very sincere. I thought that if I could only see a miracle—a real, bona fide, industrial-strength miracle—I would never have to doubt again.

I am just glad some demonic spirit didn't nudge a chair across the room. I have grown since that time. I don't need a miracle, because I have Jesus.

THE PROBLEM OF "POWER EVANGELISM"

There is another problem area when it comes to miracles. There are those who say that last-day evangelism needs "megadoses" of miracles to convince an unbelieving world. After all, seeing is believing, they say.

Is that necessarily so? In matters of faith, it may be just the opposite. At the grave of Lazarus, Jesus said to Martha, "Said I not unto thee, that, if thou wouldest believe, thou shouldest see the glory of God?" (John 11:40). That is, believing is seeing.

Yet there are those who urge us to have a miracle ministry. They are advocates of so-called "power evangelism." People who teach this approach say that power evangelism is the breakthrough for the Gospel in the unevangelized world. They are calling for a Gospel accompanied by acts of power that will convince unbelievers of the truth and will open the door wide for the Gospel.

The term *power evangelism* was coined in the 1980s at Fuller Theological Seminary in California. It describes manifestations such as healing, speaking in tongues, and deliverance from demons as tools to attract unbelievers to Christianity by persuading them of the power of Jesus.

Peter Wagner has written a book entitled *The Third Wave of the Holy Spirit*. In it he declares that the Gospel accompanied by acts of power "is what is really going to push back the veil of darkness so the lost people can hear the Gospel."[1]

Thomas Wang, chairman of the AD 2000 and Beyond Coalition of Christian Groups Committed to World Evangelism, has said, "The situation will demand that you engage in a power encounter. . . . Many of the Christians in the area will tell you that the Christian faith delivered them from the power dominion of evil spirits."[2]

Dr. Jerry Rankin, president of the Southern Baptist Foreign Mission Board, speaks of places such as India, Sri Lanka, Malaysia, Indonesia, the Philippines, Argentina, Uruguay, Brazil, and the Ivory Coast when he says, "I am convinced the people in these areas under Satan's power for these many generations will not be changed without a remarkable demonstration of the Lord's power."[3]

I want to be very careful here. I never want to appear presumptuous enough to say what God will not do, much less what He cannot do. He is God, and He can do as He pleases. I am convinced that He is doing miracles around the world and that unbelievers are being challenged by these miracles.

Yet some caution is in order when it comes to the issue of miracles and the presentation of the Gospel. Let me suggest several guidelines.

Check the facts carefully. Some Christians are so eager for something to support their faith or are so anxious to have a tool for evangelism, they may be gullible. Are the reports of miracles trustworthy? Don't be afraid to look carefully. If it cannot be tested, it cannot be trusted.

Check the focus. Does the miracle glorify Jesus, or does it glorify some man or movement? If you make too quick an endorsement, you may find yourself with egg on your face. Simon the magician and others have always wanted to use the method of miracle to make themselves look important.

Check the fruit. Are people repenting of their sin, trusting Christ, and becoming disciples of our Lord? Remember, there were crowds that followed Jesus when He turned water into wine and fed the 5,000. But there is little evidence that more than a few came to Him in true repentance and faith. It might be interesting to do some follow-up on the masses that come because of miracles.

I want to emphasize again, however, that I believe God can and does perform miracles in this day and age.

In fact, at the end of this book you will find an epilogue in which we share several stories of modern-day miracles that meet the above criteria and have been attested and recorded. I want to affirm and declare in every way the unlimited power of God to move in a miraculous way in the lives of His children when He deems to do so in accord with His purpose and His glory.

How Do You Measure a Miracle?

Miracles done by the hand of God glorify God and do not glorify men. They will validate the claims and the identity of Almighty God. They will advance God's work significantly.

If God wants to perform a miracle, He is the One who will give the faith for it. Faith is not currency that we have in our pocket to spend for whatever we want. If God wants a mountain moved, He is the One who will give mountain-moving faith.

CHAPTER THREE

WATER INTO WINE

JESUS IS GOD'S JOY FOR YOUR DISAPPOINTMENTS

* * *

Have you been keeping company with broken dreams? Does disappointment seem to be a close friend to you? Has life been unkind? Does it seem that just when it looks like the cup of joy will be filled to the brim and you can drink of it, it is instead dashed to the ground and broken?

If so, take heart. Your disappointment may indeed be God's appointment. It may be that God has a special miracle just for you. Consider this fascinating story of how God miraculously worked through what some would call a disappointment.

Shortly after the end of World War II, a young associate pastor named Cliff and his fiancée, Billie, were anxious to get married. They scraped together enough money for a simple wedding and two train tickets to a city where Cliff had been asked to hold a revival with a friend, hoping to combine their honeymoon with this responsibility.

The couple got off the train at their destination and took a bus to the hotel, only to discover that it had been taken over by the military for use as a rehabilitation center. Stranded in an unfamiliar city with only a few dollars, Cliff and Billie had little choice but to try and hitch a ride on the nearby highway. Soon a car pulled over, and the driver asked them where they wanted to go.

"We don't know," they said and explained their predicament. The driver was sympathetic and offered a suggestion. A few miles down the road was a grocery store owned by a woman he knew. She had several empty rooms upstairs and might let them stay there. The young couple was in no position to be choosy.

The woman rented Cliff and Billie a room for five dollars, and they moved in. On their first day Billie spent the afternoon practicing the piano, and Cliff played the trombone he had brought with him.

The proprietor of the store sat in a rocking chair, listening to the music. When she realized the young couple were Christians, she referred them to a friend who invited them to spend the rest of their honeymoon in his home.

Several days later the host mentioned that a young evangelist was speaking at a youth rally at a nearby Christian conference center and invited the newlyweds to attend.

It so happened that the regular songleader was sick that night, and Cliff was asked to lead music for the service. What a historic occasion that proved to be! The evangelist turned out to be a very young Billy Graham. The groom was Cliff Barrows. They met for the first time that night, and a lifelong partnership was formed.

Cliff Barrows has been a member of the Billy Graham Evangelistic Team ever since and has been used of the Lord in thousands of crusades around the world. I suppose Paul Harvey would say, "And now you know the rest of the story."[1]

God is still in the miracle-working business! It may indeed be that He has a miracle waiting for you. The same Jesus that turned the water into wine can turn your disappointment into joy.

HERE COMES THE BRIDE!

After Jesus had been baptized in the Jordan River by John the Baptist, He was ready to begin His public ministry. We might think He would choose a very auspicious, deeply religious occasion at which to launch the most important ministry that has ever taken place on earth.

But Jesus didn't do that. He and His disciples accepted an invitation and fulfilled a social obligation by attending a wedding. John tells us, "The third day there was a marriage in Cana of Galilee; and the mother of Jesus was there: and both Jesus was called, and his disciples, to the marriage" (John 2:1-2).

We pointed out in the introductory chapters that John used a word for *miracle* that means "sign." That is, the seven miracles we are going to study in this book are miracles with a message. Like road signs, they point to a destination. They give direction. They are signs with a significance. And that's true with this first miracle.

JESUS, THE LIFE OF THE PARTY

Notice the setting of this miracle. Jesus chose to perform it at a wedding, a happy occasion. Some people think it odd that Jesus would take time for a celebration, a party, at this momentous time when He was just beginning His public ministry.

But Jesus lived a life of joy. He enjoyed the festivities as much as any other guest. I am sure He shared in the joy of the bride and groom. And I have no doubt that this unnamed couple was overjoyed that Jesus had accepted their invitation.

John does not tell us the names of the bride and groom. That's significant to me. Had the Bible told us their names, that might have meant they were significant people in their culture. But evidently they were common people whose names were not well-known.

That tells me that Jesus loves ordinary people like us and is involved in the everyday issues of our lives. Here is the Lord of glory taking care of the refreshments at a party! Jesus Christ wants to be with you on Monday morning at the office just as much as He wants to be with you on Sunday morning at church.

Jesus cares about the so-called little people and little things in our lives. A small boy misquoted the Lord's Prayer by saying, "Our Father, which art in heaven, how does He know my name?" But He really does!

THE BEST ADVICE EVER GIVEN

Jesus' presence at this wedding soon turned what could have been a disaster into something delightful:

> *And when they wanted wine, the mother of Jesus saith unto him, They have no wine. Jesus saith unto her, Woman, what have I to do with thee? mine hour is not yet come. His mother*

> *saith unto the servants, Whatsoever he saith unto you, do it. And there were set there six waterpots of stone, after the manner of the purifying of the Jews, containing two or three firkins apiece. Jesus saith unto them, Fill the waterpots with water. And they filled them up to the brim. And he saith unto them, Draw out now, and bear unto the governor of the feast. And they bare it.*
>
> —*vv. 3-8*

What an embarrassment. Here is a wedding in progress with all the guests assembled, people filled with joy and laughter at this joyous occasion—and the refreshments run out. There must have been panic in the kitchen!

But Jesus was at this wedding, and He was ready and willing to do a miracle. All it took for His miracle power to be realized was for the servants to listen to Mary's advice—the best advice ever given on earth, in fact: "Whatsoever [Jesus] saith unto you, do it."

Here is the secret for any miracle. *If Jesus tells you to do something, just do it.*

Why should you and I obey the Lord Jesus Christ? Why should we learn instant, glad, full, and free obedience? Why should we follow Mary's advice to those servants at the wedding?

Reason #1:
For Our Good

We will see later that Jesus told the servants to fill six waterpots up to the brim with water, then draw out some water and take it to the master of ceremonies at the wedding feast. Those servants obeyed Jesus, and in doing so they were let in on the secret of where this wonderful new wine had come from (see v. 9, "the servants . . . knew").

If you want to be an insider spiritually, become a servant. These servants knew things that even the head of the wedding feast did not know. Why did they know and he didn't? Because servants have a way of being on the inside.

In Amos 3:7 the prophet writes, "Surely the LORD God will do nothing, but he revealeth his secret unto his servants the prophets." Servants are the ones who know the secrets.

That's true in my own office at the church I pastor, Bellevue Baptist Church in Memphis. My administrative assistant, Linda Glance, reads all of my mail. Unless someone marks an envelope for my eyes alone, she will read it first. And when I dictate a letter, Linda will know what I'm thinking and saying to people, whoever or wherever they are. Linda knows all these things because she is a faithful servant.

Look at what Jesus says to those people who serve Him: "Henceforth I call you not servants; for the servant knoweth not what his lord doeth: but I have called you friends; for all things that I have heard of my Father I have made known unto you" (John 15:15). Servants have a way of becoming friends. They have a way of moving into the inner circle.

Reason #2:
For Others' Joy

Obey Jesus not only for your own good, but for other people's gladness. When the servants obeyed the Lord Jesus and filled the waterpots (v. 7), everybody at the wedding feast was blessed by the wine Jesus had miraculously created.

I tell the people in my church they ought to pray for me in this way: "Lord, help Pastor Rogers to obey You." Why? Because when I obey Jesus, the people I minister to will be blessed. Others experience joy when we obey the Lord Jesus Christ.

Obedience is important because when our Lord does a miracle, He generally does it through others. Jesus could have performed this miracle without any human help. But He told the servants to fill the waterpots. He often does His miracles through human instrumentality.

Reason #3: For God's Glory

John tells us that by doing this miracle, Jesus' glory was manifested (v. 11).

How was His glory manifested through this miracle? He obeyed the Father, and obedience always glorifies God. Jesus said in Luke 6:46, "Why call ye me, Lord, Lord, and do not the things which I say?" What right do we have to say that Jesus Christ is our Lord and Savior if we do not obey Him? But when we obey Him, we give Him glory. That's the purpose for which we exist.

On one occasion Simon Peter and his partners spent all night fishing and came up empty. The Lord Jesus got into the boat and told Peter, "Launch out into the deep, and let down your nets for a draught" (Luke 5:4).

Peter said, "Master, we have toiled all the night, and have

taken nothing: nevertheless *at thy word* I will let down the net" (v. 5, emphasis mine). Now, Simon Peter was a commercial fisherman. He knew, humanly speaking, that it would do no good to try again. But he obeyed Jesus anyway, and the net was so filled with fish that it broke (v. 6).

I challenge you to make this the motto of your life: "At thy word." That's what Simon Peter said. Mary told the servants at the wedding to do whatever Jesus told them to do, and Jesus then worked a miracle.

Obedience to Him is always the issue. Filling waterpots may not have made sense to those servants, but they did it anyway. God's command may not make sense to you. But don't parade it by the judgment bar of your reason. Just obey. That's the secret to a miracle.

DON'T MISS THE MESSAGE

The details of this miracle are rich with symbolism. John notes in verse 6 that the six waterpots were "after the manner of the purifying of the Jews." Then after Jesus had changed the water into wine, John writes:

> *When the ruler of the feast had tasted the water that was made wine, and knew not whence it was, (but the servants which drew the water knew,) the governor of the feast called the bridegroom, and saith unto him, Every man at the beginning doth set forth good wine; and when men have well drunk, then that which is worse: but thou hast kept the good wine until now.*
>
> —*vv. 9-10*

A Picture of Joy

What is the symbolism in all of this? First, wine in the Bible is a symbol of joy. For example, Psalm 104:15 speaks of "wine that maketh glad the heart of man."

Someone may read that and think the psalmist is referring to the intoxication that strong drink brings. This is not the place to debate whether the wine Jesus created in Cana was intoxicating wine. But I don't believe that it was, because the Bible so strongly and clearly warns us against intoxicating wine.

In Proverbs 23:31 we read, "Look not thou upon the wine when it is red, when it giveth his color in the cup, when it moveth itself aright"—that is, when it is fermented. Obviously if there is a time when wine is fermented, there's a time when it is not fermented. And God's Word also calls unfermented grape juice wine.

Proverbs 23:32 contains a warning about intoxicating wine: "At the last it biteth like a serpent, and stingeth like an adder." It is unthinkable that the refreshment Jesus gives would have a serpent in it. The wine at Cana was pure wine, not polluted. Intoxication is Satan's substitute for Jesus' joy.

A Mirror of Mankind

What do the six waterpots symbolize? The Bible teaches us in Revelation 13:18 that six is the number of man.

The jars at the wedding in Cana were earthen water jars. That is, they were made of clay, just as man is made of clay (we are "earthen vessels," 2 Corinthians 4:7). So the six waterpots picture mankind.

The Rut of Ritual

Again, John 2:6 tells us that these vessels were the kind used in the purification rituals of the Jews. They were there for ritual cleansing. Mark 7 sheds light on these rituals:

> *Then came together unto him the Pharisees, and certain of the scribes, which came from Jerusalem. And when they saw some of his disciples eat bread with defiled, that is to say, with unwashen, hands, they found fault. For the Pharisees, and all the Jews, except they wash their hands oft, eat not, holding the tradition of the elders. And when they come from the market, except they wash, they eat not. And many other things there be, which they have received to hold, as the washing of cups, and pots, brazen vessels, and of tables. Then the Pharisees and scribes asked him, Why walk not thy disciples according to the tradition of the elders, but eat bread with unwashen hands?*
>
> —*vv. 1-5*

I have read that the Jews of that day would wash their hands to the elbow nine times and let the water drip off their elbows before they would eat. The idea was not sanitation but religious ceremony.

Like many of the religious rituals the scribes and Pharisees practiced, this matter of ritual cleansing had become a ceremony without meaning. So when these leaders questioned Jesus about the failure of His disciples to follow the expected procedure, He answered, "Well hath Esaias prophesied of you hypocrites, as it is written, This people honoreth me with their lips, but their heart is far from me" (v. 6).

So these waterpots represented the traditional religion of the people. They were cold clay pots, filled with ritualism, representing mankind with religion but no reality. It will be a wonderful day when people stop enduring religion and start enjoying salvation.

Filled to the Brim with Him

When Jesus told the servants to fill the waterpots, they filled them "to the brim" (v. 7). Why to the brim? Because Jesus said He had come to fulfill the law, right down to every "jot" and every "tittle," the smallest parts of the letters in the Hebrew alphabet (see Matthew 5:17-18).

All of the righteousness that the Mosaic law required was fulfilled in the Lord Jesus. Just as those waterpots at the wedding were filled to the last drop, Jesus fulfilled the law down to its last letter.

The Bottomless Well

Now I want you to follow me closely. In verse 8 of our text, Jesus gave the servants this command: "Draw out now, and bear unto the governor of the feast." Did they draw that water turned to wine from the waterpots? I think not. Those pots were filled to the brim.

I believe the servants drew the water from a well, the same well they had drawn from to fill the waterpots. My point is this: the waterpots represented the old, the law of Moses. The well represented the new, that which Jesus had come to bring.

What Jesus was saying by this action, I believe, was, "I am fulfilling the old and bringing in the new. You don't need these waterpots anymore, because you have the well. You now have Me. I have come that you might have life, and that you might have it abundantly" (see John 10:10). And did not Isaiah prophesy, "With joy shall ye draw water out of the wells of salvation" (12:3).

We know that the wine they served at the beginning of the feast was the best they had on hand, but it was far inferior to what Jesus provided later. And not only was it inferior, but it was limited. But Jesus is a well of joy marked not only by quality but by endless quantity.

After Jesus performed this miracle, that wedding had wine enough and to spare for all of the guests. The master of ceremonies gave testimony to the superiority of the wine, praising the bridegroom for what he thought was his wise planning in saving the best for last (vv. 9-10). We'll say more about that below.

Imagine the bridegroom's joy at that word. Imagine the joy of the wedding couple and their guests as they enjoyed the wine that Jesus had created by His miracle. Imagine the joy of Mary as she saw her Son exercise His divine power. And I think Jesus too was filled with joy, knowing He had brought more abundant joy to an already happy occasion.

MORE THAN ENOUGH FOR YOU!

What a wonderful picture of the abundant life Jesus came to give us. There was more than enough wine for the wedding guests. When Jesus fed the 5,000, there were twelve baskets full of food left over (Mark 6:43).

When the prodigal son contemplated returning to his father's house, he said to himself, "How many hired servants of my father's have *bread enough and to spare*" (Luke 15:17, emphasis added). When our Lord saves us, He does more than deliver us from hell. He gives us life abundant and free. He doesn't merely pardon our sin; the Bible says He *abundantly pardons*.

Suppose you mistreated somebody and then said, "Would you please forgive me?"

If the other person says, "Well, all right, I forgive you," that is a pardon. But if that one takes you into his or her arms and embraces you and begins to lavish love upon you, that is an abundant pardon. That's the kind of pardon we have in our Lord.

We also have *abundant provision* in Him. The wine was available to the guests in abundance. In Ephesians 3:20 Paul prayed, "Now unto him that is able to do exceeding abundantly above all that we ask or think, according to the power that worketh in us."

We see that in this miracle. Jesus takes hard, clay hearts filled with meaningless ritual and religion and fills them with Himself and with joy.

THE SIGNIFICANCE OF THE MIRACLE

We also need to understand the significance of this miracle, which is this: *Jesus is in the transformation business!* He transforms worthless water into sparkling wine. Jesus was in the transformation business when He walked this earth, and He is still transforming people like you and me today.

Someone wisely said, "Nature forms us, sin deforms us, education informs us, penitentiaries reform us, but Jesus transforms us." I think of how He transformed Simon Peter. Here was a blustering, burly, smelly fisherman whom Jesus changed into the flaming apostle of Pentecost.

I think of how Jesus transformed John, the author of the fourth Gospel. We think of John as the aged, tender apostle of love. But he had a hair-trigger temper in his younger days. Remember, his nickname was "son of thunder" (Mark 3:17). It was Jesus who transformed this thundering disciple into an apostle of love.

I also think of how Jesus transformed Matthew the tax collector into Matthew the apostle, chosen by the Holy Spirit to record another of the Gospels.

I think of the transformation Jesus made in the life of Mary Magdalene, out of whom He cast seven demons (Luke 8:2). She became the first human herald of His resurrection.

A man was giving his testimony at one of those old Salvation Army open-air street meetings. As he was testifying, a heckler in the crowd yelled, "Why don't you shut up and sit down? You're just dreaming."

Immediately that heckler felt a tug on his coat. He looked down to see a little girl, who said, "Sir, may I speak to you? That man who is talking up there is my daddy. Daddy used to be a drunkard. He used to spend all of the money he made on whiskey. My mother was very sad and would cry most of the time.

"Sometimes when my daddy would come home, he would hit my mother. I didn't have shoes or a nice dress to wear to school. But look at my shoes. And see this pretty dress? My daddy bought these for me." But the little girl wasn't through with that heckler yet.

"See my mother over there? She's the one with the bright

smile on her face. She's happy now. She sings even when she's doing the ironing." Then the little girl said, "Mister, if my daddy is dreaming, please don't wake him up."

I like that story because it illustrates so richly and so fully what I'm talking about. The significance of this miracle is that Jesus is the transformer. The One who turned water into wine at Cana is the One who can change radically, dramatically, and eternally anyone who will come to Him.

THE BEST IS YET TO BE

We saw back in John 2:1 that Jesus performed this miracle on "the third day." This links the miracle with Jesus' activities on the two preceding days, when He gathered about Him the core of His disciples (John 1:29, 35).

Why would the Holy Spirit inspire John to record such a seemingly incidental detail? I believe there's a hint of prophecy here that is especially significant in light of the fact that we are staring the twenty-first century—and the third millennium—in the face.

In 2 Peter 3:8 the apostle tells us, "One day is with the Lord as a thousand years, and a thousand years as one day." With that in mind, we can say that since Jesus performed this wedding miracle, there have been two days of human history. Two thousand years have elapsed since Jesus came to earth in His incarnation—two days in God's view.

Two days of history are past, and we are on the threshold of the third day. I believe this third day is about to dawn in all of its glory. And I believe that this wedding miracle Jesus performed typifies and prefigures another wedding that is coming. I'm referring to "the marriage supper of the Lamb" (Revelation 19:9). I'm looking forward to being there, aren't you?

When we sit down to that wedding feast, the wine of joy will run freely, and Christ's glory will be abundantly manifested! The wine flowed freely, and Jesus manifested His glory at Cana. But that cannot compare with the wedding feast we will enjoy when Jesus comes again in power and great glory!

That's the way it is with Jesus. It just keeps getting better and better.

We saw earlier that when the master of ceremonies at the wedding tasted the wine Jesus had miraculously made, he called the bridegroom over and complimented him on saving the good wine for last. Jesus always saves the best for the last. Satan gives us his best first.

The Bible says concerning Satan's ways, "Bread of deceit is sweet to a man; but afterwards his mouth shall be filled with gravel" (Proverbs 20:17). The pleasure of sin is only "for a season" (Hebrews 11:25). Sometimes it lasts only for a moment. Sin fascinates, and then it assassinates. It thrills, and then it kills.

If you know the Lord Jesus, however, you can sing and mean it, "Every day with Jesus is sweeter than the day before."

I will never forget hearing that chorus being sung one Sunday morning as I walked through an alley behind a Sunday school. I was in my early teens. I did not go to Sunday school because my family did not attend church. I heard the people in that Sunday school singing, "Every day with Jesus is sweeter than the day before."

I said to myself, "That is impossible. Nothing can keep getting sweeter." I did not deny that it might be sweet to know Jesus, but in my heart I did not believe what they were singing. But since I have been saved, I know it is absolutely possible and totally true.

Even though I believe I love the Lord Jesus Christ as much now as I ever have in my life, I'm looking forward to loving Him more tomorrow. I'm enjoying the wine of joy that Jesus pours out.

The Devil gives his best first, but it gets increasingly bitter as you go along. That's the way life progresses for people who don't know Christ. They begin with the wonder of childhood. Then in their youth there is vision and enthusiasm, and in young adulthood there is strength. But then in middle age, people begin to get wearied by the battle of life. And as the weariness of age sets in and things begin to deteriorate, they become bitter old people. That's why the Devil doesn't have any happy old people.

Jess Moody wrote a ways back that the famous atheist Madalyn Murray O'Hair was attempting to raise money to establish an atheist university, an atheist printing plant, and an atheist radio station. But according to Moody, the most interesting of her plans is a retirement home for atheists.

He writes:

> What do aged atheists have to talk about as they sit around to die? Do they discuss the legacy of morality, decency, integrity, and spiritual sensitivity they have bequeathed to their children? Or the good atheism has done the world: the hospitals, orphanages, the elevation of womanhood, and the mass distribution of decent literature? Perhaps they discuss the great bulwark against Communism that atheism has erected. And when the sun

> is sinking low, and when the conversation for the wheelchair atheists begins to lull, they can joyously contemplate their future. There is so much for an aged atheist to look forward to.

Of course, when atheists die, they go to hell. Without Jesus, life gets worse and worse.

Jesus' first miracle was a manifestation of His glory. But I can hardly wait for Him to come again. If you are a child of God, every pain and heartache you ever know will come on this side of the grave. Thank God that we can look forward to His coming!

NO DISAPPOINTMENT IN HIM!

When Jesus turned the water into wine, that act manifested His glory. But it was also a miracle with a message. Jesus is in the transformation business. It takes a miracle of grace to transform sinners into the children of God.

Miracles of grace are always greater than miracles of glory. Jesus turned water into wine with just a word. But to save us, He had to hang on a cross. If you're a child of God, you have already experienced the greatest miracle of all—the new birth!

YOUR RECIPE FOR A MIRACLE

Your Need—God's Joy in Place of Disappointment

- Joy in place of family disappointment.
- Joy in place of financial disappointment.

- Joy in place of physical (health) disappointment.
- Joy in place of spiritual disappointment.

God's Supply for Your Need

- The attendance of Jesus—His presence in your disappointment.
- The advice of Jesus—His word of hope for your disappointment.
- The abundance of Jesus—His bottomless well to overcome your disappointment.

How to Meet Your Need in Jesus

- *Do what Jesus says*: Take any needed step of obedience He may be calling you to take in your life.
- *Seek to gladden someone else*: Look outside yourself and your disappointments for someone who needs your help, comfort, or witness.
- *Seek God's glory*: Ask Him to use you in His service in a way that brings Him honor and glory.
- *Replace your disappointment with praise*: Thank God that you have Jesus, and that because you have Jesus, you have an abundant supply of joy and peace.

Chapter Four

A Nobleman's Son Healed

Jesus Is God's Assurance for Your Doubts

* * *

Serving Jesus with doubt in your mind is like driving your car with the brakes on. All of us wish we had stronger faith, and indeed that is what we need.

Faith is the medium of exchange in the kingdom of heaven. Jesus said, "According to your faith be it unto you" (Matthew 9:29). Years ago I heard these words: "Pray and believe, and you will receive. Pray and doubt, and you will do without."

I wanted a faith I could bank on. So for years I was on the lookout for a bona fide miracle. If I could only see a miracle with my own eyes—or touch it, or taste it, or even smell it—then my faith would be strong, so I thought.

I read about the miracles Jesus did in the Bible. I noticed that Jesus did miracles and never advertised them. Then I would see people today advertise miracles but never do them. I longed to see a miracle.

If you are like I was, hang on. The episode from John's Gospel we will examine now is just for you. You will learn that you can come to God just as you are, the way all of us come to Jesus. It was the way Charlotte Elliott came to Jesus.

Charlotte was a charming, talented, and vivacious young woman, known around Brighton, England, as "carefree Charlotte." She was a composer, an artist, a singer, and the life of the party.

But when this talented woman was just thirty years of age, she was struck with an illness that left her an invalid for the rest of her life. She became listless and depressed. One day she was visited by Caesar Milan, a well-known Swiss evangelist.

Sensing Charlotte's distress, Milan told her, "Charlotte, you must come just as you are—a sinner—to the Lamb of God who takes away the sin of the world!" Charlotte responded immediately, placing her faith in Jesus Christ for salvation. She experienced an inner peace and joy that lasted until her death at age eighty-two, in spite of her debilitating illness.

Charlotte Elliott did something special to express her joy. She wrote the great hymn "Just As I Am" to describe the joyous experience of coming to Christ just as she was and being saved.

That hymn explains how all of us must come to Jesus. We must always come just as we are, and always by faith. A certain nobleman from Capernaum learned that truth one day, and neither his life nor the life of his family was ever the same again. His story is the subject of John's second miracle (John 4:43-54).

I believe you want and need to possess a genuine faith. But there's something more important than that. You need a faith that possesses you! You need a faith that is so strong, it can hold you fast even in your darkest night of doubt or need.

That's the kind of faith the nobleman of John 4 needed. But there were some obstacles in his way. Let's learn what they were and how Jesus removed them.

THE OBSTACLES TO STRONG FAITH

According to John 4:43-45, Jesus was returning again to the region of Galilee, in particular to a town that is very familiar to us from our previous chapter:

> *So Jesus came again into Cana of Galilee, where he made the water wine. And there was a certain nobleman, whose son was sick at Capernaum. When he had heard that Jesus was come out of Judea into Galilee, he went unto him, and besought him that he would come down, and heal his son: for he was at the point of death.*
>
> —*vv.* 46-47

Here was a man with a serious problem. As a nobleman, he had prestige and power. Doubtless he also had wealth and all the perks that go with it. But he had a problem that neither his power nor his wealth could touch. His son was dying. And yet this man had some obstacles to faith in Jesus.

Obstacle #1: Secondhand Faith

The first obstacle is what I call secondhand faith. He had probably heard a lot about Jesus. That's good in itself. Everybody ought to hear about Jesus. But all this nobleman had was secondhand. All he did was listen to other people talk about Jesus' miracles.

For instance, he had heard how Jesus had changed the water into wine at Cana (v. 46). Now Jesus was back in Cana, so the nobleman went to see Him.

We know exactly what he was thinking. We would think the same thing if our child were sick. He's thinking that if Jesus could turn water into wine, maybe He could heal his sick son. So the man made the journey from Capernaum to Cana, where Jesus had performed His first miracle. There he desperately pleaded with the Lord to heal his son.

But rather than healing the man's son, the Lord seemed to remonstrate with him, almost to scold him. Jesus looked at him and said, "Except ye see signs and wonders, ye will not believe" (v. 48).

This man, however, was desperate. He would not be dissuaded. He did not want to talk theology. He simply said, "Sir, come down ere my child die. Jesus saith unto him, Go thy way; thy son liveth" (vv. 49-50a).

This man's problem was about to become the dark soil in which the flowers of faith would bloom and blossom. But secondhand faith is not strong faith. You can't go to heaven on your mother's faith, your pastor's faith, your neighbor's faith, or anybody else's faith. You can hear about Jesus and what He has done for others, but that is secondhand faith.

Jesus once asked His disciples, "Whom do men say that I, the Son of man, am?" (Matthew 16:13). He was asking for secondhand information in order to make a point.

The disciples stated what they had heard other people say about Jesus. But then Jesus asked the all-important question: "But whom say ye that I am?" (v. 15). Peter gave this ringing declaration as the spokesman for all: "Thou art the Christ, the Son of the living God" (v. 16).

That's it! They had rock-solid trust, not a hand-me-down faith.

This is the truth that the nobleman of John 4 needed to grasp. It's the truth we need to grasp as well. Otherwise, our faith will be secondhand faith.

Obstacle #2:
Sign-demanding Faith

Here's another of this nobleman's obstacles to strong faith. He had not only a secondhand faith, he had a sign-demanding faith. Jesus made that clear by His response in verse 48: "Except ye see signs and wonders, ye will not believe."

Jesus was rebuking the man. Jesus said on another occasion, "An evil and adulterous generation seeketh after a sign" (Matthew 12:39).

People were saying, "Give us a sign from heaven and we'll believe." Even when Jesus Christ was hanging on the cross, they said, "Let him now come down from the cross, and we will believe him" (Matthew 27:42).

What's interesting about this is that the "sign" these unbelievers were asking for is the same word John uses to describe the seven miracles we're studying. In other words, Jesus was doing the very signs they were asking to see.

This tells me that the problem was not a lack of believable signs. The problem was, they were demanding that Jesus "perform" for them, figuring He could not do it and then they could turn away in unbelief. Jesus never yielded to any demand like that.

"Well," somebody will say, "after all, seeing is believing." No, it is not. Believing is seeing! So many people have the idea that if Jesus would just perform a sign, everyone would believe in Him.

But the fact is, miracles are not very good tools for evangelism. Why? I think the verses that follow the miracle at Cana give us a good answer. Let's go back to John 2 for a moment:

> *Now when [Jesus] was in Jerusalem at the passover, in the feast day, many believed in his name, when they saw the miracles which he did. But Jesus did not commit himself unto them, because he knew all men, and needed not that any should testify of man: for he knew what was in man.*
>
> *—vv. 23-25*

An entourage was following Jesus because they saw His miracles and believed. But verse 24 says Jesus did not "commit" Himself to them. This is the same Greek word as the word "believed" in verse 23. The people believed in Jesus, but He did not believe in them.

Why didn't He? Because He knew these people were following Him not because he was Messiah, but because of the miracles. It was not God they were hungry for, but a sign, a miracle.

It was the same when Jesus fed the 5,000, a miracle we'll consider later. The people said, "This is wonderful. He's a walking cafeteria." But Jesus said, "Ye seek me . . . because ye did eat of the loaves, and were filled" (John 6:26).

The fickleness of their faith was proved that very day. When Jesus began to talk to them about eternal truths, eating His flesh and drinking His blood—that is, receiving Him into their lives—they began to leave Him (John 6:66). He even had to ask the Twelve, "Will ye also go away?" (v. 67).

Jesus knew man. He knew that these miracle-mongers, these people who demanded signs and miracles, did not have strong or even genuinely seeking faith. The nobleman's faith was a sign-demanding faith.

As we draw near the end of this age and the end of the twentieth century, we are going to hear more and more from people who claim to have supernatural ability to perform signs and wonders. What's wrong with asking for signs and wonders?

Signs and wonders are valid. Jesus did them. But when we *demand* signs, that dishonors God. We are then saying, "God, I can't take You at Your word. You've got to prove Yourself to me."

Suppose you are a father and you say to your son, "Son, I'm going to put one hundred dollars into a bank account for you."

Your son says to you, "That's great, Dad. But how can I be sure you put the money in the bank for me?"

"I just told you I did, son."

"Yes, I know you did. But would you mind showing me the deposit slip? I need some proof."

Do you see the insult it would be to you as a father if your word is not good enough for your child? That's what we do to God when we demand a sign. We are saying, "I need proof that You are a God who keeps His word."

I think of the doubting disciple, Thomas. The other disciples believed in Jesus and the Resurrection when they saw the empty tomb and when Jesus appeared to them. But what did Thomas say? "Except I shall see in his hands the print of the nails, and put my finger into the print of the nails, and thrust my hand into his side, I will not believe" (John 20:25).

Thomas did see Jesus a week later, and his faith was bolstered. But then Jesus said to him, "Thomas, because thou hast seen me, thou hast believed: blessed are they that have not seen, and yet have believed" (v. 29). That includes you and me!

Obstacle #3: Self-centered Faith

There was a third problem with the nobleman's faith. It was self-centered (v. 49).

What was he interested in? The welfare of his child. Is there anything wrong with that? No, just as there's nothing wrong with miracles. I promise you, if I had a child who was sick, I would be bombarding heaven with my prayers.

But here's the problem: this man has yet to bow at the feet of Jesus Christ and worship Him. So many of us are concerned only about our health, our welfare, our children, our families, and our future—but not about the will and kingdom of Jesus. That's not strong faith.

Could it be wrong to plead for the health of a child? In itself, of course not. But strong faith is interested primarily in the glory of God and a right relationship with Him.

This man was interested in the physical instead of the spiritual, the temporal instead of the eternal. The truth is, we cannot love our families as we ought until our greatest love is for Jesus Himself.

Obstacle #4:
Strong-willed Faith

Here's a fourth and final obstacle to strong faith that this nobleman needed to overcome. The faith he had was a strong-willed faith.

He seems to command Jesus. "Sir, come down ere my child die" (v. 49). As a nobleman, he was accustomed to giving orders. He was trying to tell the Lord what He ought to do, how He ought to do it, and when He ought to do it.

But notice verse 50: "Jesus saith unto him, Go thy way." Don't miss that. This man says to Jesus, "Come!" Jesus says, "Go."

Have you ever been guilty of instructing the Lord? Have you ever said, "Listen, Lord, for Your servant speaks" instead of, "Speak, Lord, for Your servant hears"? That is weak faith. Strong faith waits upon God and listens to God and gets a message from God. There's a world of difference between strong faith and strong-willed faith.

Faith is not so much receiving from God the things you want, but accepting from God the things He gives. You can't "claim it" until He names it.

Faith is not dictating to God. Faith is hearing God, believing God, and acting on what God says. This man was a nobleman. So he didn't think twice about telling Jesus what to do. But Jesus could not let his strong-willed faith go unchallenged.

THE OPERATION OF STRONG FAITH

Nothing we have said so far is meant to imply that the nobleman of John 4 was sinful or mistaken in coming to Jesus. Not at all. He was in the right place imploring the right Person. And he was about to receive a miracle.

But Jesus had more in store for this man than the healing of his son. Jesus wanted to remove the obstacles that were keeping this unnamed nobleman from developing strong faith—a spiritually revolutionary experience.

The change starts to come right in the middle of John 4:50. This man was going to get his miracle, all right, but he was also about to *go beyond the miracle to Jesus*. He was about to undergo a radical, dramatic change. I want to show you four ways the nobleman put strong faith into operation.

Hearing the Word

When Jesus said to this man, "Go thy way," He added this all-important phrase: "Thy son liveth."

As those words fell on the nobleman's ears, something began to happen to him. He heard what Jesus said. The Lord's words sank down into his heart and mind. The first trait or characteristic of strong faith is this: you must hear the Word of God.

The Bible says, "How then shall they call on him in whom they have not believed? and how shall they believe in him of whom they have not heard? and how shall they hear without a preacher?" (Romans 10:14). Paul follows that up by writing in verse 17, "So then faith cometh by hearing, and hearing by the word of God."

I don't necessarily mean that the sound waves from the spoken Word must enter your auditory canals. But in order to have faith, you must know what God has said, because faith is a response to His Word. If you want people to believe, you have to give them something to believe. And that is His Word.

Believing the Word

Having heard what Jesus said, the nobleman "believed the word that Jesus had spoken unto him" (v. 50). Hearing alone is not enough. There are people who sit in churches all across America every Sunday and hear the Word, but they have not believed it.

Someone may say, "That's my problem right there. I have trouble believing. I just can't bring myself to believe." Oh, but that's not true. A person who doesn't believe has moral problems, not intellectual problems. The problem is not in the head, but in the heart.

The Bible says, "Take heed . . . lest there be in any of you an evil heart of unbelief" (Hebrews 3:12). "The fool hath said in his heart, There is no God" (Psalm 14:1). It is not that people cannot believe. They *will* not believe. Unbelief is not weakness, it is wickedness. It is rebellion against God.

Faith is our response to God Himself, not just to what He has done. Remember, this man believed Jesus before he saw that his son was healed. He didn't see any sign or wonder. He simply took Jesus at His word.

Here was this man, looking into the face of Jesus, and Jesus said to him, "Go thy way; thy son liveth." This man was now captivated by the Person, the character, of Jesus Christ Himself. Not any sign or wonder, but Jesus.

Let me say it again: strong faith, true faith, is the response of the heart and the soul to the character and nature of Christ. It does not demand signs.

This man was now responding to Jesus, but not only because Jesus had done the miracle the man was looking for when he came. He was responding to the Person of the Lord Jesus Christ.

Obeying the Word

A third means by which we can put strong faith into operation is by obeying the Word of God. Jesus told the man to go back home, and "he went" (v. 50).

Had the man not believed Jesus, he would have stayed there still demanding a sign, still asking Jesus to heal his son. But the issue was settled, and his faith was shown by his strong obedience.

True faith, strong faith, is always linked to obedience. In Romans 16:26 Paul speaks of "the obedience of faith." And the apostle James writes, "As the body without the spirit is dead, so faith without works is dead also" (2:26). Sitting in church and taking notes is not faith. You must obey the Word.

"Well," you say, "are you telling me that I'm saved by faith and works?" No. I'm saying that you are saved by faith that works. If it doesn't work, it is not faith. Simply saying that you believe but not obeying is not faith. There's no substitute for obedience.

Resting in the Word

So this nobleman heard Jesus' word, he believed that word, and he obeyed it. But here's the sweetest part of this entire account to me:

> *And as he was now going down, his servants met him, and told him, saying, Thy son liveth. Then enquired he of them the hour when he began to amend. And they said unto him, Yesterday at the seventh hour the fever left him. So the father knew that it was at the same hour, in the which Jesus said unto him, Thy son liveth: and himself believed, and his whole house.*
>
> —*vv.* 51-53

Do you see what is happening here? Twenty-four long hours elapsed between the time the nobleman received Jesus' word that his son would live and his departure for home. I believe something wonderful was going on here.

We know this man lived in Capernaum. He encountered Jesus in Cana, about twenty miles away. He could have made that journey on foot in seven or eight hours. But remember, he was a nobleman. A nobleman wouldn't walk that far. He would go by chariot or camel or some other conveyance.

What I am saying is that if this man had left Cana immediately after meeting Jesus, he would have been home long before that entourage of his servants met him on the way. In other words, he waited a full day before leaving for home.

Let me ask you a question. If you had left home in utter desperation, seeking a miracle for your deathly ill son, and had received this word of assurance and healing from Jesus, you'd rush home as fast as you could to see what had happened, wouldn't you? So would I.

But this man waited twenty-four hours before heading home. What was happening here? I believe this is one of the most incredible demonstrations of faith in all of the Bible. It's the fourth way we can put strong faith into action: by resting in the

Word. This man's faith was now so strong that he remained an extra day, resting in Jesus' word. There was no reason to hurry.

The Bible says, "He that believeth shall not make haste" (Isaiah 28:16). You don't have to worry. You can wait on the Lord. "Rest in the LORD, and wait patiently for him" (Psalm 37:7). You don't need to get all upset and go around in nervous exhaustion. Rest in the Lord. Commit your way to Him (Psalm 37:5).

Now why did Jesus do this miracle this way? Why didn't He go with the man and heal his son? Because He was after more here than just a physical healing, as important as that was. He was building this father's faith.

So while this man did not have the physical presence of Jesus at his son's bedside, he had something just as wonderful. He had the word of Jesus. When you need a blessing, when you need an answer to prayer, do you have to have Jesus there with you physically to get it? No. That boy was twenty miles away, but Jesus healed him anyway.

The psalmist writes of the Lord, "He sent his word, and healed them" (Psalm 107:20). Jesus is not with us in body today, but we can hold His Word in our hands.

Jesus was saying to this desperate father, "It does not matter whether I go to your home or not. Just take Me at My word."

How wonderfully significant that is. We must remember that Jesus has gone back to heaven in His literal body. Therefore, He cannot stand by my bedside or the bedside of one of my loved ones and heal them. Then too, if He were still here and came to my house, then He could not be at yours at the same time.

Remember that Mary had the same problem with the absence of Jesus, even when Jesus was here on earth in a literal body (in

Chapter 9 we will study this miracle). Her brother Lazarus grew sick and died, and Mary's complaint was, "Lord, if thou hadst been here, my brother had not died" (John 11:32).

And yet by the ministry of the Holy Spirit who represents Jesus to each of us, I have all of Jesus there is to have in me, and so do you. By the Spirit and the Word of God, we have something far better than the literal presence of Jesus doing signs and wonders.

So when I have my Bible with me in my study, it's like having Jesus in my study. When I open my Bible at home, it's like having Jesus at home with me.

Someone may object, "You're worshiping the Bible." No, I don't mean it that way. I'm saying that when I pick up the Word of God and read it, God speaks to me from His Word. Faith is finding a promise in the Word of God, brought home to your heart by the Spirit of God, and standing on it.

THE OBJECTIVE OF STRONG FAITH

Here is the final truth I want you to see from this wonderful account in John 4. Let's consider the objective of strong faith.

> *So the father knew that it was at the same hour, in the which Jesus said unto him, Thy son liveth: and himself believed, and his whole house. This is again the second miracle that Jesus did, when he was come out of Judea into Galilee.*
>
> —*vv. 53-54*

John says the father believed when he realized that Jesus' word was absolutely true. But verse 50 says he had already believed the day before, when Jesus announced his son's healing.

The Discovery of Faith

What's the difference in these two verses? In verse 50, the man believed Jesus for the healing of his son. In verse 53, John makes it clear that the nobleman was believing unto salvation. Now he was believing not just in a miracle, but in a Messiah. *He had gone beyond the miracle to Jesus.*

I can picture this man as he goes home, gets out his Old Testament Scriptures, and calls out to his wife, his son, and the rest of his household, "I have found the Messiah! We must believe on Him and be saved."

That's why Jesus performed His miracles. They are "signs" that point to Him, so that we might *go beyond them and believe in Him.*

The Necessity of Faith

Now we know the full story behind this "second miracle" that John records. Jesus not only wanted this man to believe in Him, but He wanted the man's entire family to be saved.

That's the true bottom line, isn't it? What lasting good would have been accomplished if Jesus had merely healed this boy, only to have him grow up, die years later, and go to hell? Jesus didn't heal everybody. But He saves everybody who calls upon Him. He did not come to be a Teacher or a Healer. He came to be our Savior.

Jesus said of Himself, "The Son of Man is come to seek and to save that which was lost" (Luke 19:10). We know that Jesus sometimes healed large numbers of people. He fed thousands on two different occasions. The Bible never says that all of those people were saved. Many probably never came to true faith in Christ.

That tells me it is possible to be the recipient of a miracle and yet still be lost. That's why Jesus did not major on miracles.

I was praying with a woman in a hospital room one day. I must have been praying loud enough for others to hear (my wife says I cannot whisper), because a woman called out from across the hall, "Come see me too."

I thought she was calling for a nurse, so I just went on with my visit. But she called out again, "Come see me too."

So I went over and asked her, "Are you talking to me?"

"Yes," she said. "I want you to come see me." So I went into the room across the hall and found a precious lady lying on the bed.

I can still see her in my mind. Her white hair was spread out on the pillow. Pain was on her face. Despair was in her heart. I could tell by the look on her face that she had very little time left to live. Her face was ashen gray. The smell of death was in that room.

She said, "I'm not ready to meet God. Mister, can you help me?"

I said, "Yes, ma'am, I can." And I told her about the Lord Jesus and His death on the cross for her sins. Then I said, "If you will trust Him, He'll save you."

She said, "Would you help me?"

I led her in the sinner's prayer, and she repeated every word after me. When I said amen, she said amen also.

I opened my eyes, expecting to see the peace of God on her face. But instead I saw a tortured look. She said, "I don't see how just saying that can do any good."

"You're right," I replied. "Just saying the words won't do any good at all. It is believing in Christ that saves you. Let's pray again—and this time, really put your faith in Jesus."

We prayed the prayer again, and she said, "Lord, I really trust You." Then I saw the peace of God come over that precious woman's face. I expect to meet her in heaven.

That's what these miracles in John's Gospel are all about. Believe in the miracles, but trust in Jesus!

YOUR RECIPE FOR A MIRACLE

Your Need—God's Assurance in Place of Doubt

- Assurance in place of secondhand faith.
- Assurance in place of sign-demanding faith.
- Assurance in place of self-centered faith.
- Assurance in place of strong-willed faith.

God's Supply for Your Need

- The assurance of His presence (Hebrews 13:5).
- The assurance of His Word (Psalm 119:89).

Jesus wants to give you strong faith in place of doubt. He wants your faith to be:

• *First-person instead of secondhand,* so you won't have to depend on someone else's experience.

• *Open-handed instead of sign-demanding,* so you won't try to dictate terms to Jesus.

• *Christ-centered instead of self-centered,* so you won't settle just for what you want, but for what Jesus wants for you.

• *Self-surrendering rather than strong-willed,* so you won't try to tell Jesus what to do.

How to Meet Your Need in Jesus

To experience the strong faith Jesus wants to give you:

• *Hear the Word*: You need to know what God has said. Open your Bible and read it for yourself.

• *Believe the Word*: Respond in trust to what God has said.

• *Obey the Word*: Act on your belief. Do what God tells you to do.

• *Rest on the Word*: When you have done what God wants you to do, rest in the confidence that He will do exactly what He said.

CHAPTER FIVE

HEALING THE IMPOTENT MAN

JESUS IS GOD'S STRENGTH FOR YOUR DISABILITIES

* * *

Each morning my wife, Joyce, gives me brewer's yeast, apple cider vinegar, bee pollen, and a handful of vitamins. In addition, it's my goal to walk two miles each morning. What a way to start a day!

Despite all that, I am learning that my strongest ability is my disability. Father Time and Mother Nature are not very kind parents.

Alas, such is the nature of human flesh. One of my friends in years past was Paul Anderson, called "the world's strongest man." One sports announcer called him "a wonder of nature" when Paul was winning weight-lifting titles. He won an Olympic Gold Medal for weight-lifting in 1956. Paul is also in the *Guinness Book of World Records* for an unbelievable feat of strength: lifting more than three tons with his back.

Paul Anderson was a stellar athlete and an outstanding Christian, with a vibrant testimony for Christ. But his kidneys began to fail him, and he died at the age of sixty-one. The strongest man on earth could not keep his body from winding down to the grave.

If Jesus doesn't return, you and I will eventually taste physical death, no matter how much strength or health we have. The statistic on death is, one out of one dies.

The Bible says in Isaiah 40:30, "Even the youths shall faint and be weary, and the young men shall utterly fall." All human strength will utterly, ultimately fail. But the Bible also offers us this glorious word of hope: "Though our outward man perish, yet the inward man is renewed day by day" (2 Corinthians 4:16).

There is no "fountain of youth" for the body, but there is one for the soul!

The great question, therefore, is not, what is going to happen to your body? The great question is, do you have the inner spiritual strength to be what God wants you to be?

John 5:1-14 tells of the healing of a paralyzed man, and this miracle points us to the inner strength that Jesus alone can give. Spiritually, if you have fallen and can't get up, read on. There is healing for your spiritual paralysis and incredible power for victorious living.

A Health Spa for the Soul

In verse 1 John links this miracle with the healing of the nobleman's son in the previous chapter. "After this" looks back to what has just occurred. Having dealt with human doubt, Jesus now prepares to deal with human disability.

After this there was a feast of the Jews; and Jesus went up to Jerusalem. Now there is at Jerusalem by the sheep market a pool, which is called in the Hebrew tongue Bethesda, having five porches. In these lay a great multitude of impotent folk, of blind, halt, withered, waiting for the moving of the water. For an angel went down at a certain season into the pool, and troubled the water: whosoever then first after the troubling of the water stepped in was made whole of whatsoever disease he had.

—John 5:1-4

Let's begin by seeing the setting of this miracle. The word *Bethesda* means "house of mercy," and the poor man we are going to meet was about to experience the mercy of God in a miraculous way as the Lord Jesus passed his way.

I have often visited this pool in Jerusalem. It's right inside the sheep gate (v. 2; the word "market" is not in the original). The pool is still there, about forty feet below street level now.

In Jesus' day, the pool of Bethesda was something like a health spa. The porches around the pool were full of sick people, men and women with all kinds of serious maladies (v. 3). They were there waiting and hoping for a miracle. Apparently once a year, when the water was stirred up, God in His mercy would perform a miracle of healing on the first person who stepped into the water.

Why Doesn't Jesus Heal Everybody?

Jesus came to Jerusalem during an unspecified feast and went to the pool of Bethesda. There He fixed His attention on a "certain man" who had been an invalid for thirty-eight long years (v. 5).

There were many sick people there, but Jesus focused on this man because He had a purpose in mind and a lesson to teach. He was about to perform a miracle with a message for us.

We don't know exactly how long this man had been lying beside the pool of Bethesda, waiting for the troubling of the waters. It's possible he had been coming every year, trying to inch closer so he could be the first in the water and be healed.

Jesus knew all about the man's condition, so He asked him a very simple but profound question. "Wilt thou be made whole?" (v. 6). That's a question Jesus is still asking today, because this man's condition is representative of the spiritual condition of untold numbers of people today.

Before we examine this miracle, it's important to remember that Jesus was not merely in the healing business. The Bible says a great multitude of sick people was there that day, but Jesus only healed this "certain man."

As a matter of fact, we are going to learn that after this healing, Jesus silently slipped away (v. 13). Had He stayed, the people would have clamored after Him to be healed.

If Jesus were interested in being a great Healer, He would have gone from person to person and healed them all. But He healed just one man because He was teaching a great spiritual truth of which the healing was a symbol. Jesus did not come as the great Healer. He came as the great Savior.

In the introduction I referred to G. Campbell Morgan's observation that every parable Jesus taught was a miracle of instruction, while every miracle that Jesus wrought was a parable of instruction.

Morgan didn't mean the miracles were not real. He was saying there is a message in each miracle. That's the premise of this book, and we can see it here in the miracle at Bethesda. Jesus healed the invalid in order to get a message across to all of us who are spiritually "impotent," without strength.

That's all of us, because by nature we are paralyzed and without strength apart from Jesus. But in Him we can have power for living because Jesus is God's answer to our spiritual disability.

Physical and Spiritual Healing

Let me say something else by way of introduction to this story in John 5. The physical healing of this invalid was only temporary. He still died, perhaps not too many years later since he had already been sick for almost forty years. The point is that the physical healing really was at best temporary.

If we are sick, we want to get better. I know I do, and so do most people. But if you have noticed, in the average church prayer meeting the requests for prayer are often like this: "Pray for Sister Druggers. The doctor says she may be in critical condition. Pray for Deacon Cooper. He has cancer and isn't doing well," etc.

Well and good! If I'm sick, I want people to pray for me. But how many prayers are offered for the lost in the community, that they may be saved, or for fallen brothers and sisters in Christ, that they might be restored? And how many times do we intercede for ourselves and others concerning the spiritual health and vitality we need for our own spiritual disabilities?

We think recovering our health is all-important, but God

doesn't always think it's as important as we think it is. He may have a different and a greater plan for us.

We have an example of this in Mark 2:1-12. This is the story of the paralyzed man who was brought to Jesus by four friends carrying him on a stretcher. They let him down through the roof of the house to Jesus, who looked at him lying there and said to him, "Son, thy sins be forgiven thee" (v. 5).

When Jesus said that, the religious experts in the crowd began to criticize Him. They said in effect, "Who does He think He is? Only God can forgive sin" (vv. 6-7).

They were right about that! And to prove they were right, and to prove who He is (v. 10), Jesus said to the paralyzed man, "Arise, and take up thy bed, and go thy way into thine house" (v. 11). Jesus healed him in order to attest to the greater spiritual miracle He had just performed in forgiving the man of his sins.

Jesus did something the people could see so that they might understand and believe that which they could not see. The important thing to Jesus that day was not healing the man's body, but healing his soul. The physical healing did not last forever. This man died too. But the spiritual healing of his soul will last for eternity.

ARE YOU READY FOR A MIRACLE?

So it was with the man at the pool of Bethesda. Let's go back to John 5 and learn three things we need to do if we are going to experience the power of God over our disability. Here is the message in the miracle for us today.

Validate Our Weakness

The first thing we must do if we would find the strength this man found so long ago is to admit that we are weak.

The fact that this man was lying by the pool of Bethesda was an admission of weakness. It wouldn't have done him much good to deny his illness. When you are physically unable to move under your own power, your lack of strength is evident to all. The man readily admitted to Jesus that he was too weak to make it into the pool on his own (v. 7).

But the problem with many of us today is that we will not admit we are spiritually paralyzed. We will not validate our weakness. Even if we can hide spiritual paralysis from others, we cannot hide it from God. The first step in being healed from spiritual weakness is to admit it.

In Romans 5:6 Paul writes, "For when we were yet without strength, in due time Christ died for the ungodly." The Bible describes every person without Christ as being "without strength."

Even as believers, we often get the idea that while we needed Jesus to save us, we can live the Christian life in our own strength (the old Adamic nature).

But our flesh is as sinful and weak now as it was before we came to Christ. Jesus did not come to remodel our sinful nature or to remove it, but to give power over it. Therefore, if we try to live in the strength of the flesh, it should not surprise us that we are spiritually weak. Here are three truths we cannot deny and cannot dodge.

The primary source of our weakness. What causes spiritual weakness? The answer is in John 5:14: "Afterward Jesus findeth him in the temple, and said unto him, Behold, thou art made whole: sin no more, lest a worse thing come unto thee."

The primary source of this man's weakness was his sin. Not everybody is sick because of sin, but evidently this man was. I think that's the reason Jesus picked him out. The man's sin and his weakness had a direct connection, or else Jesus would not have given him such a direct warning.

We are sinners by birth, sinners by nature, sinners by choice, and sinners by practice. The source of all spiritual disability is, to put it bluntly, sin! We may try to rename it—mistake, misjudgment, psychological maladjustment, glandular malfunction—anything but sin. But the problem will persist until we with absolute honesty confess our sin.

The paralyzing force of our weakness. Many people do not realize they are spiritually paralyzed. I'm not talking about physical or intellectual or financial weakness. I'm talking about spiritual paralysis.

We saw above in Romans 5:6 that Christ died for those who are weak, whom Paul calls the "ungodly." Do you know what our weakness is? Our weakness is that we don't have the strength to be godly.

We were created to reflect the image of the Creator. Godliness is, simply put, reflecting that image and the glory of God. Therefore, sin is coming short of the glory of God (Romans 3:23). Sin, the gap between our lifestyle and the glory of God, is the source of our weakness.

What is God's plan for me and for you? God's plan is that we be godly, that we be holy just as He is holy (1 Peter 1:16). But we don't have the strength within ourselves to be godly. I don't care how hard you try, you don't have what it takes to be godly. And neither do I.

We may be strong enough to do as we want, but we're not strong enough to do as we ought. The primary source of our weakness is sin, and the paralyzing force of our sin is that we cannot be what God would have us to be.

The persistent course of our weakness. According to John 5:5, this man at Bethesda had been in his condition for thirty-eight years.

When a person is paralyzed for that many years, his muscles begin to atrophy and wither. Every year that this man was sick, he was getting worse, not better. His muscle tissue was deteriorating.

So it is for people who are without Christ. The longer they live, the worse their condition becomes. That's the reason no one should put off giving his or her heart to Jesus Christ.

But the process of atrophy also affects believers like the ones we talked about above. They are the ones trying to live for Christ in their own strength—or we should say, in their own weakness. Their attempts to be godly in the flesh weaken them further. The man who struggles in quicksand sinks all the more.

Once the paralyzing force of sin takes effect, the course of the disease is persistently downward. If we want the spiritual healing the man of Bethesda received, we must validate our weakness. We must say, "Dear God, You are right. I am without strength. I lay my pride in the dust and admit my need to You."

Activate Our Will

If we want God to replace our disability with His strength, we must also activate our will.

Let me take you back to John 5:6, to the question Jesus asked the impotent man: "Wilt thou be made whole?" In other words, Jesus was asking him, "What is your will in this matter?" He wanted the man to activate his will.

God will never make you choose His way. He will enable your will but not coerce it. If God were to coerce you, if your relationship with Him were forced, you'd no longer be a person—you would be a machine. And God can have no fellowship with machines.

I recently saw this bumper sticker: "The more I learn about women, the more I love my truck." I hope he didn't mean it.

In activating our will, notice first there is a question to answer, a choice to be made. If you want to come to Christ, you may. But if you don't want to come to Christ, He will not force you. The very last invitation in the Bible is this: "Whosoever will, let him take the water of life freely" (Revelation 22:17). Jesus cried out at the great Feast of Tabernacles in Jerusalem, "If any man thirst, let him come unto me, and drink" (John 7:37).

Those are marvelous invitations. But if you don't want to come to Christ, God will not allow even one of the angels in heaven to drag you to Him.

However, if you want to come, there are not enough demons of hell to keep you from coming. God has given you a will. So Jesus said to the man at the pool of Bethesda, "Do you want to be whole?"

Now I know I'm heading into a theological minefield here. Many theologians react to the idea of human free will because they think it negates the sovereignty of God.

But I believe in both because I believe that both the sovereignty of God and the free will of man are taught in Scripture. The fact that God respects human will does not negate or denigrate His sovereignty at all. There are many truths of Scripture that we hold in tension because our teacup minds are not big enough for God's ocean of truth.

There's an old story about a room full of preachers who were having a discussion on theology. They got into a heated argument over the sovereignty of God and the free will of man. Some said, "Nobody can choose God. God does the choosing. From eternity, He has predestined some for heaven and some for hell. Salvation is the sovereign work of God from beginning to end."

But other preachers said, "Wait a minute. The Bible says that whosoever will may come and that the Lord is not willing that any should perish, but that all should come to repentance."

The argument got so heated, the preachers separated into two holy huddles. On one side of the room were those who argued for the sovereignty of God. On the other side were those who argued for the free will of man.

But one poor man was caught in the middle. He just couldn't make up his mind. When he heard the "sovereignty" preachers talk, they sounded so right. But when he heard the "free will" preachers give their case, he thought that sounded good too.

But he had to choose, so he chose the group that argued for the sovereignty of God and against human free will. These preachers saw him coming and asked, "Why did you come over here?"

"Well," he said, "I just chose to. I came of my own free will."

"Then you don't belong in this group," they told him. "Go over there with those fellows."

So the befuddled preacher went over to the other group. But

they saw him coming and asked, "Why are you coming over here?"

"They sent me over here. It wasn't my choice."

So the second group said, "You can't come over here unless you come of your own free will."

Those are the kind of silly arguments that people get into. But I want to tell you that God never made any person for the purpose of going to hell. People who go to hell are there as intruders. Jesus tells us that hell was "prepared for the devil and his angels" (Matthew 25:41).

Is God sovereign? Surely He is—sovereign enough to give a person a will without losing His sovereignty. But here in John 5 the Lord is teaching us that He will not force Himself upon any individual.

Now it's true that this man could never have said yes to Jesus except Jesus first gave him the initiative. "We love him, because he first loved us," the Bible says (1 John 4:19). God does not force our will, but He does enable our will. We could never choose Him if He had not first chosen us.

But that fact does not negate our responsibility to choose. Jesus' question to the crippled man at the pool of Bethesda was therefore a valid question: "Do you want to be made whole?"

So there is not only a question to answer—there is *a choice to make*. Why would Jesus ask a sick person if he wanted to be whole? The answer seems obvious; the question itself seems superfluous.

But Jesus wasn't just asking him if he wanted to walk again. He used a word for *whole* that means basically "fullness, wholesomeness." Jesus was offering this man more than a strong pair of legs. He was offering him spiritual as well as physical wholeness; He was offering the forgiveness of sin.

This man had a choice to make. Many people want the results of sin erased, but they don't want to give up their sin. They don't want to be made truly whole. They don't want the pardon that God offers them.

This happens sometimes on the human level. Every so often we hear of a criminal who refuses an offer of clemency. One of the strangest cases on record was that of George Wilson, who was sentenced to be hanged in 1829 by the state of Pennsylvania for mail robbery and murder.

Before the sentence could be carried out, President Andrew Jackson pardoned George Wilson. The presidential pardon was sent to the governor of Pennsylvania and then to the warden of the penitentiary where George Wilson was incarcerated. There the message was given to the condemned man.

But Wilson stunned everyone by refusing the pardon, even though he knew it meant the death penalty would be carried out. The officials didn't know what to do. They couldn't just take Wilson to the front door of the prison and push him outside. It was a real legal tangle.

The case ended up in the U.S. Supreme Court. In rendering the court's decision, Chief Justice John Marshall said, "A pardon is a piece of paper, the value of which depends on its acceptance by the person implicated. If it is refused it is no pardon." As a result, George Wilson was hanged even though a pardon had been offered. He had made his choice.

A person can die and go to hell even though Jesus stretches out His arms to that person and asks, "Will you be made whole?"

A pardon that is refused is no pardon. We must activate our will to receive what Jesus offers.

Do you really want victory? You need not persuade our Lord to give it to you but must merely permit Him to do so.

Initiate Our Walk

Here's a third thing we must do if we would have our disability replaced by Jesus' strength. We must initiate our walk. Let's consider verses 7-9 of our text:

> *The impotent man answered him, Sir, I have no man, when the water is troubled, to put me into the pool: but while I am coming, another steppeth down before me. Jesus saith unto him, Rise, take up thy bed, and walk. And immediately the man was made whole, and took up his bed, and walked: and on the same day was the Sabbath.*

Remember that the purpose of the miracles in the Gospel of John is to teach us greater spiritual lessons and to point us to Jesus. John did not write his Gospel so that paralyzed people might be healed. He wrote it so that lost people might be saved and have abundant life. He wrote it that we might receive strength from above, so that by believing in Jesus we can walk in vitality, liberty, and victory day by day.

Notice that Jesus not only offered this man a choice, but He commanded him to do something. Jesus did not help him to his feet and fold up his mat for him. The man had to initiate his walk. Now getting up and walking did not cause the man to be healed.

He was healed by the power of Christ. But walking demonstrated that he was whole.

The spiritual principles at work here are so clearly laid out in Ephesians 2:8-10, Paul's classic statement of salvation:

> *For by grace are ye saved through faith; and that not of yourselves: it is the gift of God: not of works, lest any man should boast. For we are his workmanship, created in Christ Jesus unto good works, which God hath before ordained that we should walk in them.*

Those three marvelous verses are built around three key prepositions: *by*, *through*, and *unto*. The order here is important. You can't rearrange the sequence. Let me show you how these prepositions and the truths they teach apply to what Jesus told the lame man at Bethesda.

How was this man made whole? *By grace*. There was nothing he could do. He was paralyzed. He could not help himself physically (John 5:7), or spiritually either. But the Bible says he was immediately made whole. Salvation is by the sheer grace of God.

Imagine that you and I were standing there that day and heard Jesus' command. We might be saying to each other, "This isn't right. Jesus shouldn't taunt that poor crippled man. How can He tell him just to get up? If he could have walked, he would've done so a long time ago. Jesus is being impossible, unreasonable." But while we're talking, the man is getting up!

Jesus Christ does what is humanly impossible and humanly unreasonable because with Him all things are possible. He can save a sinner against all possibility and all reason because salvation is by grace.

Salvation, Paul says in Ephesians 2:8, is also *through faith*. The crippled man exercised his faith when he obeyed Jesus' command to get up, take up his bed, and walk away. Again, getting up didn't make him whole. He was made whole by the grace of God. But he still had to exercise faith by initiating his walk.

Jesus was saying to the crippled man, "Just obey Me. Just trust Me." So the man put his faith into action and got up. Faith is belief with legs on it.

Ephesians 2:10 says we are saved *unto good works*. That is, we are saved for the purpose of doing good works. The verb Jesus used in telling this man to get up and walk is a verb of continuous action, not just a single step. It means to walk and keep on walking.

Was this man healed because he walked, or did he walk because he was healed? He walked because he was healed. We are not saved by doing good works, but we are saved to do good works. Salvation is *by grace, through faith, unto good works*. You can't get that out of order and make it work.

Jesus is the answer to your disability, and to mine as well. That's why we must *go beyond the miracle to Jesus*. We cannot live the Christian life until we receive Christ. Then the Bible says, "As ye have therefore received Christ Jesus the Lord, so walk ye in him" (Colossians 2:6).

How did we receive Christ? By grace through faith. How do we walk in Him? The same way. Once you understand that, you will receive the strength to live supernaturally. God will replace your disability with His ability.

As great as the miracle of John 5 is, I need to remind you again that Jesus did not come as the great Healer; He came as the great Savior. He came as God's remedy for our spiritual disability. This miracle is given to underscore that truth.

WHY WE FOLLOW CHRIST

To close this chapter, I want to share a remarkable letter that a wise man wrote to his daughter. She has given me permission to share it with you. It's entitled, "Why I Follow Christ":

> I have not seen clear statistical evidence that fewer Christians die of cancer than nonbelievers, or that they are immune in greater degree from the diseases that afflict the human race. Some of the kindest, most selfless persons I know have had more than their share of bad health. The fact that they belonged to Christ did not insulate them from disease. Therefore, I will not follow Christ for promised healing.
>
> I will not deny or dispute evidence of restoration of health. I will rejoice at every recovery from what seems to be hopeless, threatened death. I will not hesitate to pray for recovered health for my loved ones and acquaintances. I will set no limits on what God may do. But I will not follow Christ for promised healing.
>
> I see no sign that Christians escape disaster and accident more often than others. I have helped dear friends empty muddy water out of dresser drawers and new appliances after a disastrous flood. I remember as a child taking clothes to a widow with five children whose house had burned to the ground. A bullet makes no detour around the body of a believer. Therefore, I will not follow Christ for any promised protection from disaster.
>
> I will not scoff at amazing survivals, nor deny that providence

has and continues to work for the good of God's own. I will continue to pray for protection from wicked men and tragedy, but I will not follow Christ for promised protection from accident or catastrophe.

I do not observe that Christians are especially favored with prosperity. Like James, we have all seen the rich oppressing the poor, and justice is rarely perfect in this world. The psalmist has said that he had not seen the righteous forsaken or his seed begging bread, and in the deepest needs of this life that is certainly true; but all of us have known people of integrity who have not been prospered. Therefore, I will not follow Christ for promised freedom from physical want or the hope of affluence.

I am not certain that Christians have stronger personalities or fewer neuroses than nonbelievers. I do know that there is no bitterness like religious bitterness and no arrogance more insufferable. I have watched Christians suffer emotional and mental disabilities. And though it may seem heretical, I am not sure that I would really enjoy living in the same house with either the apostle Peter or Paul.

God wills that the mind of Christ be formed in us, and there is no doubt in my mind that the Christian's attitudes and actions will be improved by his Christianity. But I will not follow Christ for any promise of personality enhancement or perfection.

Why then follow Christ? Why be a disciple of Jesus when life may become more complicated, as He so often warned?

For one reason alone. In Jesus we behold the face of God. He is the truth, the everlasting truth, God in the flesh. I know that in His life, death, and resurrection I am reconciled to God, the Giver of life. I believe that nothing can separate me from the love of God. He has all power and goodness. I trust Him in His promises.

To Him I offer my life, damaged or whole, brief or full of years. It matters not. He is the one certain thing in an uncertain world. He is to be worshipped, not so something will happen to me or to the world (something already has happened to me and the world), but because He is God, who through Christ has reconciled the world to Himself. He saves me; He is my justification; He is the center that holds.

To worship the God of our salvation, to offer sacrifices of praise and thanksgiving, that alone is our vocation. We offer our lives to God, not so as to be healthy, wealthy or wise; not even so as to gain strength to do great things for Him. We offer our lives to Him because He alone has claim on us. God is not a means.

Do you see what this man is saying? We do not follow Christ so He can perform miracles or do wonderful things for us, but because He is the Son of God who reconciles us to Himself.

In this day of New-Age mysticism, religious charlatans, and the "happiness boys" preaching health and wealth on television, we had better get a lock on Jesus Christ. If we will admit our weakness, activate our will, and initiate our walk by coming to Him in faith, we will find Him to be the answer to our disability.

YOUR RECIPE FOR A MIRACLE

Your Need—Strength for Your Disabilities

You must validate your weakness.

- Admit that the problem is sin.
- Recognize that you need to receive Christ as your Savior, or,

• If you are a believer, recognize the weakness of your flesh, your inability to live for Christ in your own strength.

You must activate your will.

• Answer the question, "Do you want to be whole?"

• Make the choice to receive Jesus' forgiveness and pardon.

You must initiate your walk.

• Don't stay where you are; get up and come to Jesus.

• Accept His forgiveness and receive His strength by faith, through grace.

God's Supply for Your Need

Strength for your physical disabilities: God does choose to heal some people of physical illness and affliction.

Strength for your spiritual disabilities: God has healing for everyone who will admit their spiritual paralysis and come to Him. He has:

• Salvation for the sinner (Romans 6:23; 10:13).

• Strength for the believer (Philippians 4:13).

How to Meet Your Need in Jesus

• *Admit your need for Jesus*: for salvation, if that is your need, or for the strength to live the Christian life.

• *Bring your disabilities to Jesus*: Bow before Him, and lay your sin and weakness at His feet.

• *Trade your disabilities for His strength*: If you are coming to God for salvation, receive Him by faith. Salvation is God's gift to you (Ephesians 2:8-9). If you are a Christian, remember that you live for Christ the same way you received Him—by grace through faith (Colossians 2:6).

• *Get up and walk*: Get ready to serve God in the power of the Holy Spirit (Ephesians 2:10).

CHAPTER SIX

FEEDING THE 5,000

JESUS IS GOD'S SATISFACTION FOR YOUR DESIRE

* * *

Every time I read about Jesus' great miracle of the feeding of the 5,000, I remember what happened one time when I traveled in the Holy Land with a group of friends.

We were scheduled to visit the place where Jesus performed this miracle. I thought it might be good to remind the people of that, so I asked my guide, "Would you please get me two fish and five loaves of bread?"

I planned to go up on the mountainside and have everyone sit down. Then we would break the loaves and divide the fish and let everyone have a taste, just to remind ourselves of the miracle Jesus did.

I had the lunch all ready that day, but things didn't work out quite like I planned. The night before, we had had an exotic Arabic meal. It was a wonderful meal, but it was filled with all kinds of foods that American stomachs are not accustomed to.

When we got up early the next morning, the sun was blazing

hot. We started out across the Sea of Galilee in a boat, reenacting Jesus' trip. The water was choppy, and our boat went up and down on the waves. It was so hot, I felt like I was wearing a lead coat. Are you starting to get the picture?

Our people were beginning to sag and droop, but I thought when I fed them the bread and fish they would perk up. So we arrived at the place, and I found a stone table. At the right moment, I unwrapped the loaves and the fish.

One man in our group came to the table and looked down at that bread and fish. Just then a fly walked across one of the fish. He said something to me I'll never forget—"If everyone feels like I do, you could feed 5,000 with that!"

Fed Up But Not Fed

What's the moral of the story? There comes a time when the things of this world are not enough. There comes a time when we are fed up with the things of this world and need far more than bread and fish.

We learned that in a rather humorous way that day near the Sea of Galilee. But 2,000 years ago Jesus had a serious and eternal message to deliver through His miracle. The message is that He is the answer to man's desire.

Blaise Pascal, the great physicist and philosopher, said there is a God-shaped vacuum in the heart of every person that can only be filled by Him. There is in every human heart a hidden hunger for a right relationship with God, and that can only come through Jesus Christ. Jesus is God's answer to our deepest desire.

NO PROBLEM TOO BIG TO SOLVE

In John 6 we learn that a great crowd was following Jesus and the disciples as they crossed the Sea of Galilee:

> *After these things Jesus went over the sea of Galilee, which is the sea of Tiberias. And a great multitude followed him, because they saw his miracles which he did on them that were diseased.*
>
> —*vv.* 1-2

When Jesus arrived at His destination, thousands of people were there waiting for Him. They were hot, tired, and hungry, and there was not a McDonald's in sight. This was a big problem, considering the number of people involved.

John says that Jesus looked up and saw this great crowd coming toward Him. He knew the people did not have any food. We are told in Matthew 14:15 that this was a "desert place" and that it was late. So Jesus asked Philip, "Whence shall we buy bread, that these may eat?" (v. 5).

Knowing Where to Turn

Now Philip knew they had a problem too, because Jesus had laid it in his lap. He told Jesus, in effect, "Why, it would take almost a year's wages just to give everyone a mouthful of food" (v. 7).

Why did Jesus ask Philip that question? Was the Lord seeking advice? Was He in a panic? No. Verse 6 tells us that Jesus already knew what He was going to do.

I had lunch one day with a grand Christian woman who is now in heaven—Corrie ten Boom, the courageous woman who, with her family, rescued Jews from the Nazis in Holland and wound up in a concentration camp. Corrie said to me that day, "There is no panic in heaven, only plans."

Jesus knew what He was going to do with all of those hungry people. The holy Trinity never meets in emergency session. Jesus wasn't asking for advice, nor was He trying to learn about Philip. He already knew all about Philip. He knows all about all of us (John 2:25). Jesus wanted Philip to learn something about Philip, and about Himself.

Philip had it all calculated. He knew how much it would cost to feed the crowd. His answer was a good one in that it was accurate. But it was a bad answer because Philip left Jesus out of the equation. He gave the kind of answer any good, red-blooded atheist could give.

We're all guilty of leaving God out of our calculations sometimes. We say, "Well, I have a problem here, and it looks impossible. This is what it's going to take to solve it." But we forget to include the Lord Jesus. That's sad, because there is no problem too big for Him to solve.

Using All Our Strength

One day a little boy was trying to turn over a big rock as his father watched, bemused. The little fellow was grunting and straining and heaving, but he couldn't turn the rock over.

His dad asked with a whimsical smile on his face, "Son, are you using all of your strength?"

"Yes, Daddy, I'm using all my strength."

"No, you're not. You haven't asked me to help you. I'm your father, and my strength is your strength."

Sometimes we wrestle with problems and say, "I don't know what to do. I'm at the end of my strength." That's just what God wants us to say. Jesus was trying to get Philip to see that his problem may have been too big for him, but it wasn't too big for Jesus.

Take your most serious problem and double it. Now double it again. Is it too big for God? Of course not. "I am the LORD, the God of all flesh: is there any thing too hard for me?" (Jeremiah 32:27). Put this in your heart and mind, and get it down big, plain, and straight: *there is no problem too big for Jesus to solve.* Do you believe that? I hope you do.

NO PERSON TOO SMALL TO USE

Here is a second truth I want you to see in this miracle: *there is no person too small for Jesus to use.* Jesus uses people to solve problems, and on this occasion He used a little boy.

"One of his disciples, Andrew, Simon Peter's brother, saith unto him, There is a lad here, which hath five barley loaves, and two small fishes: but what are they among so many?" (vv. 8-9). Evidently Andrew was out talking with the crowd, and he found this boy with his lunch.

Not only was this lunch small in amount for so many people, but it was meager. These were small fish, probably like sardines. And barley was the coarsest and the poorest of bread. And not only was the supply tiny, but its bearer was just a young lad. What could he accomplish?

This was the lunch of the poor, but the Lord Jesus used it to bless a multitude. What was the recipe for this miracle?

Transferred to Jesus

First of all, the boy gave all of his lunch to the Lord. He didn't say, "Jesus, You can have one of these fish, and I'll keep the other one. Take three of these loaves, but let me keep two. I'm hungry."

Do you want to be used of God? Well, have you given everything to Him? You say, "Now, wait a minute. He doesn't expect me to give Him everything."

I beg to differ. God asks you and me to *give Him everything we are and have*. In fact, the person who tries to hold on to his life is the one who loses it. Jesus said, "Whosoever will save his life shall lose it; but whosoever shall lose his life for my sake and the gospel's, the same shall save it" (Mark 8:35).

That little boy gave his entire lunch to Jesus, but do you think he went away hungry? He had more to eat than if he had not given Jesus anything. When he gave it all to Jesus, Jesus gave back to him.

You cannot outgive God. "Give, and it shall be given unto you; good measure, pressed down, and shaken together, and running over, shall men give into your bosom" (Luke 6:38). This boy's lunch was transferred to Jesus.

Taken by Jesus

When you give Jesus something, He will receive it. Even if it is just a cup of cold water given in His name, He'll receive it. There is no gift too small for Him to use.

Jesus only asks of you what you have, not what you don't have. When Mary gave that sweet perfume to the Lord Jesus to anoint His feet before His burial, He said of her gift, "She hath done what she could" (Mark 14:8).

All of us can do what we can do. You may think that's an obvious statement, but we often forget it. God asks you to do what you can. He asks you to give what you have, not what you do not have. Jesus took the boy's meager lunch and performed a miracle with it.

Transformed by Jesus

Don't insult God by saying He cannot use you. God specializes in taking ordinary people and doing extraordinary things with them. The Bible says, "Not many mighty, not many noble, are called: but God hath chosen the foolish things of the world to confound the wise" (1 Corinthians 1:26-27).

Think again of Mary and her act of devotion to Jesus at Bethany. Jesus said of her, "Wheresoever this gospel shall be preached throughout the whole world, this also that she hath done shall be spoken of for a memorial of her" (Mark 14:9). The world is still filled with the perfume of Mary's gift because it was transformed by Christ into a perpetual memorial.

I think also of the widow in Mark 12:41-44 who came to the temple and put in her two mites—"all her living," according to Jesus (v. 44). It was all she had, but because she gave it to the Lord, He transformed it into a gift that was more than anyone else gave.

There were many rich people bringing their gifts that day. But Jesus said she gave more than all of them. He delights to take ordinary people and do extraordinary things through them. He took a little boy's lunch and proceeded to feed a crowd with it (vv. 10-13). You may be too big for God to use, but you'll never be too small for God to use.

NO HUNGER TOO DEEP TO SATISFY

Here is the third truth I want you to see in this miracle: *there is no hunger too deep for Jesus to satisfy*. The miracle He did that day is significant not because He fed 5,000 people, but because through it He taught us that He can meet the deeper, spiritual hunger of our hearts.

This is where we find the message in the miracle, the significance of the sign. This is where we *go beyond the miracle to Jesus Christ Himself.*

Jesus Is Spiritual Bread

We are told in John 6:14-15 that Jesus had to leave the scene of His great miracle because the people wanted to make Him king by force. In other words, He was not able to teach any lesson in connection with the miracle because the people were in no mood to listen.

The teaching came the next day, when the people came looking for Jesus again: "When they had found him on the other side of the sea, they said unto him, Rabbi, when camest thou hither?" (v. 25).

They had been searching for Him because they thought they had found a perpetual cafeteria, a "bread" Messiah. But Jesus said, "Verily, verily, I say unto you, Ye seek me, not because ye saw the miracles, but because ye did eat of the loaves, and were filled" (v.26).

When Jesus says "Verily, verily," that means put your antenna up. Pay close attention. He knew the only reason these people had tracked Him down was because He'd fed them. They wanted bread and fish. So He gave them, and us, a very important command:

> *Labor not for the meat which perisheth, but for that meat which endureth unto everlasting life, which the Son of man shall give unto you: for him hath God the Father sealed. Then said they unto him, What shall we do, that we might work the works of God? Jesus answered and said unto them, This is the work of God, that ye believe on him whom he hath sent.*
>
> —*vv.* 27-29

This is what it's all about, that we believe on the Lord Jesus Christ. Jesus is spiritual bread. We need to see beyond the temporary things of this world, "the meat which perisheth."

People have said to me, "Why did you build that big church building? Why didn't you take that money and feed the poor instead?" You may have had a similar charge thrown at you by those who can't see past the material.

I say to people like that, "Why did the banker build that big building? Why did they have to build that football stadium? Why don't they sell that stadium and use the money to feed the poor? Why don't they sell the gas station on the corner and use the money to feed the poor?"

"Well," the person may say, "people need money, and they

need recreation. And they certainly need gasoline." But let me tell you, people need Jesus more than they need anything.

Our world has the idea that all people need today is the food that perishes. But if I had five billion dollars and spent it to buy every person on earth a snack, in several hours they would all be hungry again. Food perishes.

It is valid and necessary to feed the poor. And we will be blessed when we help the helpless. We ought to do that. But the problem with the so-called social gospel, as opposed to the saving Gospel, is that the social gospel puts an emphasis upon that which is temporary. The saving Gospel emphasizes that which is eternal.

Some people are only interested in making the world a better place to go to hell from. What we must do is to get people saved. They need more than soup and soap. They need salvation. They need Jesus Christ. Jesus said to the people who came to Him, "I am the true spiritual bread. Don't come because I fed you bread. Come because I can satisfy your deepest hungers."

You have an eternal, never-dying soul. Jesus is spiritual bread. He is what your soul hungers for.

Jesus Is Supernatural Bread

Not only is Jesus spiritual bread, He is supernatural bread. In John 6:30 the people said to Jesus, "What sign showest thou then, that we may see, and believe thee? what dost thou work?" They were asking Jesus to do a performance for them. They were saying, "Work a miracle. Do a little celestial magic for us."

Jesus only performed His miracles to teach, never as publicity stunts. He never did miracles in order to attract followers per se. The fact is that these same people who followed Him when He fed the 5,000 left Him when He began to talk to them about eternal realities (v. 66).

Miracles are not the best form of evangelism. This same crowd that had just seen an incredible miracle was now asking for another miracle, because people cannot be satisfied by miracles. The only thing that satisfies is a right relationship with God through Jesus Christ.

Now notice what the crowd said:

> *Our fathers did eat manna in the desert; as it is written, He gave them bread from heaven to eat. Then Jesus said unto them, Verily, verily I say unto you, Moses gave you not that bread from heaven; but my Father giveth you the true bread from heaven.*
>
> —*vv. 31-32*

Manna was bread supernaturally provided from heaven to the Israelites. All they had to do was go outside and pick it up.

But here Jesus says that manna was not the true spiritual bread. It was only an illustration of the true bread. He was saying, "I am the true bread you hunger for. My Father has sent Me from heaven to feed your souls."

In verse 33 Jesus made what He was talking about perfectly clear: "The bread of God is he which cometh down from heaven, and giveth life unto the world." He was talking about his heavenly origin.

The manna that came down from heaven was a prophecy of Christ—a type of Him. It came down from heaven; He came down from heaven. It lay upon the ground; He was meek and lowly of heart. It was round, which speaks of His eternality. It was white, which speaks of His purity. The manna had the taste of honey, which spoke of His sweetness. It was flavored with oil, which spoke of the anointing that was upon the Lord Jesus Christ. It gave them life—it sustained the people physically; Jesus sustains us spiritually.

Old Testament manna pictured the Lord Jesus Christ. It had to be appropriated in order to sustain physical life. And Jesus must be appropriated—personally received—if we would have eternal life. Jesus is heaven's bread.

When the people heard this, they said, "Lord, evermore give us this bread" (v. 34). But they did not understand. In fact, soon they would forsake Him who is heaven's bread provided for their deepest hunger.

Jesus Is Satisfying Bread

Now we come to the message in the miracle. Here is why Jesus fed 5,000 people. "Jesus said unto them, *I am the bread of life*: he that cometh to me shall never hunger; and he that believeth on me shall never thirst" (v. 35, emphasis added). Jesus is satisfying bread for our souls.

People are searching everywhere for satisfaction, but they'll never find that satisfaction until they seek it in the right place—Jesus.

You may say, "I can't get any satisfaction. When I get one thing I think I want, it doesn't satisfy me. So I get something else, but it doesn't satisfy either." That will always be true, because satisfaction can only be found in the Lord Jesus Christ.

Jesus Is Sustaining Bread

The final truth we need to learn from the miraculous feeding of the 5,000 is this: Jesus is sustaining bread.

> *Verily, verily, I say unto you, He that believeth on me hath everlasting life. I am that bread of life. Your fathers did eat manna in the wilderness, and are dead. This is the bread which cometh down from heaven, that a man may eat thereof, and not die. I am the living bread which came down from heaven: if any man eat of this bread, he shall live for ever: and the bread that I will give is my flesh, which I will give for the life of the world.*
>
> —*vv.* 47-51

If there were a food or vitamin available that would allow people to live to be 100 and enjoy good health, some people would kill for it. They would do anything to sustain life.

But Jesus says that if we feed on Him, the bread of life, we will never die. We will have everlasting life.

I attended Stetson University in Florida, not far from Ponce de Leon Springs. Ponce de Leon was the Spanish explorer who came to Florida and thought he had found the fountain of youth. He was searching for water that a person could drink and enjoy perpetual youth.

There is no fountain of youth for the body, but there is one for the soul. It is Jesus. Paul wrote, "Though our outward man perish, yet the inward man is renewed day by day" (2 Corinthians 4:16). Jesus is the bread that sustains life.

Why did Jesus feed 5,000 people that day? To meet their needs, because He had compassion on them. But more than that,

He performed this miracle to teach us that He is the bread of life, and that if we will feed upon Him, we will live forever.

We must *go beyond the miracle to Jesus*. The people He fed that day were hungry again the next day. But those who seek Jesus, who feed on Him, are perpetually filled, satisfied, and sustained. Jesus said in John 10:10, "I am come that they might have life, and that they might have it more abundantly."

SEEKING JESUS

We saw earlier that Jesus said, "Labor not for the meat which perisheth, but for that meat which endureth unto everlasting life" (v. 27). Again, Jesus said in the Beatitudes, "Blessed are they which do hunger and thirst after righteousness: for they shall be filled" (Matthew 5:6).

What you need to hunger for, what you need to thirst for, what you need to seek, is righteousness. You say, "Adrian, I thought you just said we need to seek Jesus."

That's right. You need to seek Jesus. But to seek Jesus is to seek righteousness, because Jesus is made unto us "wisdom, and righteousness" (1 Corinthians 1:30).

Seek Jesus Preeminently

When Jesus told us to hunger and thirst after righteousness, that was another way of saying, "I am what you hunger for. I am the righteousness and the satisfaction your soul really needs."

The word *blessed* means "joyful, happy, satisfied." But Jesus did not say, "Blessed are those who hunger and thirst after blessedness."

That's what is wrong with the world today. Everybody wants to be blessed. "Bless me, Lord. Give me joy. Give me satisfaction," is the cry of our day. But people who seek satisfaction and joy never find it.

Why? Because satisfaction and joy are by-products of a right relationship with Almighty God. Jesus said those who hunger and thirst after righteousness are those who will be truly happy.

The lack of satisfaction, the sense of unfulfilled desire that permeates our world, is only a symptom of a greater sickness, which is unrighteousness.

Suppose you have a fever and pain. You go to the doctor, who gives you something to deaden the pain and bring down the fever. That's fine as far as it goes, but suppose the doctor never deals with the infection that is causing your fever and pain. That doctor is not practicing good medicine.

This is what many people today are trying to do spiritually. They simply want to deaden the pain of their unhappiness and misery rather than deal with the disease of unrighteousness that is causing the pain.

Let me say it again: what we need is the Lord Jesus Christ. We are to hunger and thirst after Him, and when we do that, we find blessedness.

You see, you will never need anything else spiritually besides Jesus. You should seek nothing more, and you should settle for nothing less—not a denomination, creed, church membership, or moral code.

You'll never be satisfied until you have Jesus Christ in your heart. You can't go beyond Jesus. You need to go beyond the miracles to Jesus, but there is nothing else beyond Him. You may go deeper *into* Jesus, but you'll never go *beyond* Jesus. The Bible's message is: *believe in the miracles, but trust in Jesus.*

Sometimes people ask me, "Adrian, have you received the second blessing?" I say yes, and then they say, "Well, tell me about it."

I answer, "The second blessing is discovering what I got in the first blessing. And not only have I received the second blessing—I've had the third blessing, which is discovering that I didn't learn it all in the second one."

I think you see my point. There is always more and more to learn about Jesus, but Jesus is what we need—all that we need. We need to seek Him preeminently.

What are the people of this world seeking? We might include on this list food, fashion, fitness, fame, and friends. There is nothing wrong with these in their place. But what is their place? Second place. God demands and deserves first place. When you put things first and God second, you're never going to have your heart hunger satisfied.

Seek Jesus Purposefully

We also need to seek Jesus purposefully. Jesus said in John 6:27 that we are to labor for the things that endure forever. This means to be intense about it, to be serious about it. God does business with those who mean business. The reason some people go away spiritually hungry is that they have no appetite for Jesus.

You can tell when people are truly hungry. They will take

food on almost any terms. I've seen men in big cities eating out of garbage cans. I've seen people humble themselves for food.

When a man is truly hungry, he'll beg for food. His desires are very narrow. He's not interested in the next football game or basketball game or anything else. If a man is starving, he's reduced to one desire. He wants food, and he'll humble himself for it.

Suppose you prepared a sumptuous feast for a guest in your home. You went all-out to prepare a meal that was as visually appealing as it was delicious.

But then your guest sits down and announces, "I'm not going to eat." When you ask what's wrong, he says, "Well, my plate is chipped. The parsley is on the wrong side of the plate. And I see a spot on the tablecloth."

Right away, you know two things about this person. He's rude, and he's not really hungry. A hungry person will not quibble about the placement of the parsley!

Have you ever known people who go to church to criticize the program? They don't like this, they don't like that. They have a list of things that bother them.

You can go to any church seeking something to criticize and find it. But if you go seeking Jesus, you will find Jesus. Hungry people are humble people. They're not there to criticize. They are there to feast on Jesus. They want to be fed. How hungry are you?

Seek Jesus Perpetually

Look again at John 6:35, where Jesus said, "He that cometh to me shall never hunger; and he that believeth on me shall never thirst."

We are to seek Jesus perpetually, continually. If we do this,

Jesus says we will never be hungry or thirsty again. Does that mean we will eat once and never want to eat again? Of course not.

I believe Jesus means that every time you are hungry, He will be there to feed you. Every time you are thirsty, He will be there with the water of life. Your hunger will never go unsatisfied if you will come to Jesus. He is saying, "I will give you a continual appetite for Me, and I will give you continual satisfaction of your appetite."

When a man doesn't have an appetite, he's either sick, dead, or fed. Now there are times, such as Thanksgiving, when people sit down about three inches from the table and eat until they touch the table. They get up from the Thanksgiving table around two or three o'clock and say, "I'm so stuffed, I don't care if I ever eat again." They are totally satisfied.

But what happens about eight o'clock? They find themselves out in the kitchen, looking in the refrigerator for that turkey wing.

Why is that? God made us that way. If we are healthy, we have a continual appetite. The same is true with the things of Christ. He gives us a continual appetite so that we might be continually satisfied with Him. You just keep on feasting and feasting on Jesus.

Whenever you hunger for Jesus, He will be there with the satisfying bread of His presence. Whenever you thirst, He will be there with living water. Hallelujah! What a Savior we have in the Lord Jesus Christ.

Your Invitation to the Banquet

Did you notice what Jesus said in John 6:50-51? All we have to do to enjoy the bread of life is to sit down at the table and eat!

Invite a hungry person to sit down to a banquet, and you won't need to invite him twice. The banquet I've been describing is Jesus' banquet. I'm not the chef; He is. He is the One who says to you, "Come and eat."

But you have a choice to make. You can come to the Word of God—to Jesus, and say, "No, thank You. I'm not hungry," and go away empty.

Or you can say, "Jesus, You are what I need. You are what I hunger for. I want You."

You say, "Adrian, that's what I want. How do I feed on Jesus?" Let me point you back to Jesus' word in John 5:24: "Verily, verily, I say unto you, He that heareth my word, and believeth on him that sent me, hath everlasting life."

If you will bring your faith to the Word of God and receive Christ, if you will seek Jesus and feed upon His Word, if you will bring your hungry soul to Him, the same Lord who has satisfied me for more than four decades will satisfy you.

I can promise you on the authority of His Word that you will have a continual feast and perpetual satisfaction in Jesus. The banquet table is set. Come and eat!

YOUR RECIPE FOR A MIRACLE

Your Need—God's Satisfaction for Your Desire

God's Supply for Your Need

Remember, there is no problem too big for God to solve.

- Know where to turn—bring your problem to Jesus.

• Use all your strength—ask God for His help.

Remember, there is no person too small for God to use.

• Transfer what you have to Jesus, no matter how small your "lunch."

• Jesus will accept what you have—that's all He expects from you.

• Jesus will transform what you have.

Remember, there is no hunger too deep for God to satisfy.

• Jesus is your spiritual bread—He is sufficient for your deepest hunger.

• Jesus is your supernatural bread—sent down from heaven.

• Jesus is your satisfying bread—you will never need any other.

• Jesus is your sustaining bread—the supply will never stop.

How to Meet Your Need in Jesus

To experience God's supply, you must seek Jesus.

• *Seek Jesus preeminently*: Take a hard, Holy Spirit-guided look at your life. What do you really want more than anything? If your honest answer is something other than Jesus, ask God to change your desire.

• *Seek Jesus purposefully*: What is it you want and need Jesus to do for, in, and through you? Take time to think through and answer this question. Be specific as you bring your request to Jesus.

• *Seek Jesus perpetually*: Have you lost your spiritual stamina? Are you no longer hungry for Jesus? He is always ready to satisfy your hunger. Pray for a renewed and increased spiritual appetite.

• *Accept His invitation to the banquet*: Sit down at the table with the One who can turn a boy's lunch into a feast. Nourish your soul on Jesus and never go hungry again!

CHAPTER SEVEN

CALMING THE STORM

JESUS IS GOD'S PEACE FOR YOUR DESPAIR

* * *

In this chapter I want to introduce you to an old friend. You've known him for a long time, I suspect, but you probably did not know he was a friend.

What is a friend? A friend is somebody who makes you a better person. The Bible says, "Iron sharpeneth iron; so a man sharpeneth the countenance of his friend" (Proverbs 27:17). This means that a true friend will put an edge on your life. A true friend will make you a sharper person.

Sometimes a friend will love you so much, he will hurt you in order to help you. "Faithful are the wounds of a friend; but the kisses of an enemy are deceitful" (Proverbs 27:6).

How would you like to have a friend who would help you live a clean life and draw you closer to Jesus? How would you like to have a friend who would give you more spiritual strength and help you win your loved ones to Jesus Christ? How would you like to have a friend who would make you a mature believer in the Lord Jesus?

Well, you already have a friend like that, and we are about to meet him in John 6. His name is Trouble. Now Trouble may seem like a strange friend, but Trouble can do all of these things for you if, in the midst of your trials, you will allow the Lord Jesus Christ to do His perfect work in you.

In the miracle we are about to consider, Jesus' disciples got into trouble—big trouble. But Jesus had a miracle with a message for them, a message we desperately need to hear and heed today.

If your life is sailing along smoothly right now, I'm grateful (and so are you). But you need to know that when the storms come, you can go to Jesus and find in Him an anchor for your soul.

For the fifth of Jesus' sign miracles in the Gospel of John, we need to turn back to John 6 and pick up the verses that immediately follow the miracle we just studied, the feeding of the 5,000.

In John 6:15-21 we are going to move from the hillside above the Sea of Galilee into the middle of the sea itself. From this vantage point, we are going to learn that just as Jesus is able to satisfy our deepest hunger, He is also able to reach us in our deepest despair. This is the message of the miracle for us today.

As we study this wonderful story, I want to give you six truths about Jesus Christ that will anchor your heart and life when the storms of life come. These six truths, these six anchors, will keep you steady and help you ride out the storm.

I want to help you discover that Jesus is God's answer to your deepest despair. Through this miracle we are going to learn six wonderful lessons that will remind us of the need to *go beyond the miracles to Jesus*. Let's look at the trouble, and then at the miracle.

GOVERNED BY HIS PROVIDENCE

The first thing you need to know when you find yourself in a storm is that you are governed by God's providence. This storm surprised the disciples, but not Jesus:

> *When Jesus therefore perceived that they would come and take him by force, to make him a king, he departed again into a mountain himself alone. And when even was now come, his disciples went down unto the sea, and entered into a ship, and went over the sea toward Capernaum. And it was now dark, and Jesus was not come to them. And the sea arose by reason of a great wind that blew.*
>
> —*vv. 15-18*

As we know, Jesus had just fed the 5,000. The crowds were clamoring after Him because of the miracle He had performed. Their stomachs were full, and they wanted to make Him a king.

Sailing into a Storm

But Jesus had no interest in being that kind of a king, so He withdrew to a mountain to pray and to get away from the clamoring miracle-mongers. Before He did so, He sent His disciples down to the water to go across the Sea of Galilee.

I suppose my favorite place and time in the land of Israel is by the shore of Galilee in the evening. There's a little hotel with a wharf that goes out into the Sea of Galilee. I enjoy sitting on that wharf, watching the sun reflect on the water as it sets on the Golan Heights.

That setting is so tranquil, so quiet. The birds are flying over the water, and you can feel the gentle breeze. It's so beautiful, it's almost intoxicating to sit there and enjoy the Sea of Galilee at evening. I can see why the old rabbis used to say that God made all the other bodies of water, then made the Sea of Galilee just for Himself.

The reason I mention that is that John says it was evening on the Sea of Galilee when this miracle took place. It was that beautiful and tranquil time of day. The last thing the disciples expected that evening was trouble.

I can just picture the scene. The moon is there in the night sky, like a gardenia pinned on the lapel of the night. I can feel the gentle breeze as it kissed the disciples' cheeks, like the kiss of a baby. These were seasoned sailors who set sail that evening because the Lord had told them to do so.

As a matter of fact, we are told in Matthew 14:22 that Jesus "constrained" the disciples to get into the boat and set out for the other side. This trip was His idea. So the disciples left, little aware that trouble was ahead.

They were so full of joy and peace that evening. They had just seen their Master feed 5,000 people. They were filled with a sense of exhilaration and power. After all, their Master was a miracle-worker. Besides that, they had eaten themselves and were filled with bread and fish. And yet they were unknowingly sailing into the teeth of a storm.

Sailing by Jesus' Order

You've been there, haven't you? Everything seems to be serene and beautiful. You're sailing along, like the disciples were that night. Then the storm of adverse circumstances hits.

Those winds that can sweep down so suddenly on the Sea of Galilee arose that night. Huge waves reached up to devour them, and water was filling the boat. The wind was contrary. The moon was hidden. Suddenly it was very dark.

Matthew gives us a few details about this miracle that add to our understanding of what was happening. This storm hit during the darkest part of the night, between three and six o'clock in the morning (14:25).

The disciples were rowing, and their backs were aching. Their hands were paralyzed with fear, but they couldn't stop because they were out in the middle of the sea. They couldn't go back, and it was difficult to go forward. It was too far to swim to the shore, and besides, the shoreline was lost in the inky blackness. They were filled with despair.

But their plight was fully known to Jesus. It is impossible that the One who created the seas, who has the power to still the waves, and who can walk on water would be surprised by a storm. The Bible says, "He commandeth, and raiseth the stormy wind, which lifteth up the waves thereof" (Psalm 107:25).

As we have already seen, this entire incident was ordered by the Lord Jesus. He was the One who sent the disciples into the storm. They were not there because they were out of the will of God. They were there because they were in the will of God.

Perhaps you are in the eye of a storm right now. It looks like your little boat is sinking. The icy waves are reaching up for you. It's so dark, you cannot see your hand before your face. Every wind of circumstance seems to be contrary to you.

But I want you to know, there is nothing that comes to you

except that which Jesus either causes or allows. One way or the other, you are being guided by His providential care.

You may not be able to see Jesus in your darkness, but He has His eye upon you. Whether we can see it or not, whether we understand it or not, the fact is, God has not relinquished His rule over the universe. Your storm is not beyond His control.

GROWING BY HIS PLAN

Here is a second truth, a second anchor for your soul, that emerges from the miracle of Jesus walking on the water. Even when the storm is at its worst, you are still growing by His plan.

What is God's plan for you? God wants to enlarge you, not indulge you. God is not nearly as interested in making you happy and healthy as He is in making you holy.

Growing Through Trouble

Think about the times when you have grown the most, when you have been developed and enlarged spiritually. Were they not the times when your friend Trouble came along? It's in the storm that we are stretched and enlarged.

We spend a lot of time trying to avoid trouble. No one really enjoys having trials, but we need to realize the truth that God often puts us in the middle of affliction to develop us. The Lord Jesus engineered this storm for His disciples. David testified, "Thou hast enlarged me when I was in distress" (Psalm 4:1).

I can tell you that I have grown the most in my own life during times of deepest despair. I know that when my wife, Joyce, and I watched our little baby boy step over into heaven very suddenly one Sunday afternoon, we grew a quantum leap. I know that when one of my daughters went through deep heartache and distress, God stretched my heart and life.

I would never want those things to happen again, but they did happen. And I'm a better person because of those trials. The poet has said:

I walked a mile with pleasure,
She chatted all the way,
But left me none the wiser
For all she had to say.

I walked a mile with sorrow,
And not a word said she.
But oh, the things I learned from sorrow
When sorrow walked with me.

Isn't that true? We are enlarged when we are in distress. Faith, like film, is developed best in the dark. I don't know why that is, but it is true. The plan of God for your spiritual growth and mine includes storms and trials.

Breakfast of Champions

I think of the time Israel came to the border of Canaan and sent out the twelve spies to spy out the land. Joshua and Caleb were two of those spies, and they brought back a good report. But the other ten spies put fear in the hearts of the people (Numbers 13:26-29, 31-33).

They said, "Well, it's a bountiful land, filled with milk and honey and all kinds of good things. It has wonderful hills and valleys, and you can dig iron out of those hills. But there are giants in the land. We saw the sons of Anak there. They're so big, we felt like grasshoppers. We can't take the land."

Right in the middle of this report, Caleb spoke up and said, "Let us go up at once, and possess it; for we are well able to overcome it" (Numbers 13:30). But the others drowned out his voice, and the people pulled back.

More than that, they became angry at Moses for bringing them out of Egypt (Numbers 14:3). I love what Caleb said in verse 9: "Rebel not ye against the LORD, neither fear ye the people of the land; for they are bread for us."

What did Caleb mean by that? What happens when you eat bread? You get strong; you grow. Caleb was saying, "These difficulties are there to make us grow. These people are bread for us. We can take the land. These Anakim are just the 'breakfast of champions' for us."

Dear friend, you will never grow until you eat the bread that God sets before you. Often that bread is trouble. To grow spiritually, you have to have difficulty. It is part of God's plan to grow you up in Christ.

Graced by His Prayers

Not only are you governed by God's providence and growing by His plan when you are in the storm, but you are also graced by His prayers.

Jesus went up to a mountaintop alone after sending His disciples out into the sea (John 6:15). Do you know what He was doing up there? He was praying (Matthew 14:23).

A Perfect View

From that mountaintop, Jesus had a perfect vantage point. He saw the clouds as they began to roil and boil. He saw the sea as the waves began to rise. He saw the disciples rowing desperately. He saw the whole thing (Mark 6:48).

Jesus saw it all, and He was praying. The disciples may not have known that Jesus had His eye upon them, but He did. They couldn't see Him, but He saw them. He never took His eye off them. And there on that mountain, Jesus was interceding for them. They were graced by His prayers.

His Eye on You

Are you in the midst of a storm? If so, you can say, "His eye is on the sparrow, and I know He watches me." Jesus is watching over you, and He is praying for you.

The Bible says, "He is able also to save them to the uttermost that come unto God by him, seeing he ever liveth to make intercession for them" (Hebrews 7:25). Sometimes we ask other people to put us on their prayer list or they make the same request of us. We may or may not remember to pray for these people, because we are finite and forgetful and we cannot pray for everyone and everything. If you try to do that, your prayer life will become a stagnant swamp rather than a controlled river.

I pray for a lot of people, and when somebody tells me they

pray for me every day, tears generally come to my eyes. If you have somebody on earth praying for you, you are blessed.

But think of it. You are on Jesus' prayer list! He knows you. The hairs of your head are numbered. You're not an incident or an accident. God not only loves us all; He loves us *each*. Jesus was right there praying for the disciples as they entered the eye of the storm. They couldn't see Him, but He could see them.

GLADDENED BY HIS PRESENCE

The fourth "soul anchor" I want to show you in this miracle is found in John 6:19-20:

> *So when they had rowed about five and twenty or thirty furlongs, they see Jesus walking on the sea, and drawing nigh unto the ship: and they were afraid. But he saith unto them, It is I; be not afraid.*

Remember, it was now the darkest hour of the night. These men were afraid. But it was in the darkest hour that Jesus came.

Forgetting the Miracle

Why did He not come sooner? Was He being cruel? Was He wanting them to suffer? I can imagine the disciples with their backs aching, looking into the mouth of a watery grave, asking, "Where is Jesus? Why doesn't He come help us? If He could feed 5,000 people, He could surely save us."

But Jesus had His eye on them all the while. He had been praying for them the whole time. The problem was not that He had forgotten them. It was that they had forgotten Him. That is, the disciples had already forgotten the true significance of the miracle by which He fed the 5,000. The Gospel of Mark tells us:

> *He went up unto them into the ship; and the wind ceased: and they were sore amazed in themselves beyond measure, and wondered. For they considered not the miracle of the loaves: for their heart was hardened.*
>
> —*6:51-52*

Mark is not saying the disciples had forgotten that the miracle happened. They just forgot what it was all about.

You may remember that after the miraculous feeding, the disciples gathered twelve baskets full of fragments. I believe the disciples took those baskets into the boat with them. So there was every man with a basket full of bread and fish right between his feet in the boat. But the Bible says they forgot the miracle of the loaves. They forgot that the Lord who could feed a multitude with a poor lad's lunch could keep their boat from sinking.

This is why you and I need more than miracles to live on. We need Jesus. How easily we forget the miracles. We're like sports fans who cheer their hero when he wins the game today but boo him when he blows the game tomorrow. Miracle-producing faith never lasts. We always want another miracle.

Here were the disciples saying, at least in their hearts, "Give us another miracle." But what they needed was not another miracle. They needed the Miracle-worker, the Lord Jesus Christ Himself.

Jesus waited for some time before He came to the disciples and stilled the storm. He came to them at exactly the right time, but from our perspective He waited quite a while. So the question naturally arises, why didn't He come earlier? Why did He delay?

Jesus' Gracious Delays

The answer is found in Isaiah 30:18:—"Therefore will the LORD wait, that he may be gracious unto you." Many times the Lord will deliberately delay, in order to be gracious to us.

When Jesus' beloved friend Lazarus was sick, his sisters sent for Jesus to come and heal him. But John tells us that rather than coming immediately at the family's request, Jesus waited until Lazarus had died (John 11:1-11).

We will consider John 11 later in this book, but I want to make a few observations here. In verses 14-15 Jesus told His disciples that Lazarus was dead and that He was glad He was not there.

Why would Jesus say that? Because He had something greater in mind than healing Lazarus of his illness. Suppose the Lord had come earlier and laid His hand upon the fevered brow of Lazarus, healing him instantly. Lazarus would have been just one more person that Jesus healed.

Someone could have said, "Lazarus might have recovered anyway. People do get better sometimes. How do we know this was a miracle?"

We need to keep the context of John 11 in mind. Jesus was not on His way to Jerusalem to be received as King. He was on His way to die (see v. 16).

So a healing could have been questioned. But when a person raises the dead, no one can say it might have happened anyway! Jesus had a greater plan, which was the greater glory of God.

God waited 4,000 years to fulfill His promise to send the Lord Jesus into this world. But the Bible says that Jesus came "when the fulness of the time was come" (Galatians 4:4). God is never late, never ahead of time, never in a hurry.

He always comes at just the right time to gladden us with His presence. "The vision is yet for an appointed time, but at the end it shall speak, and not lie: though it tarry, wait for it" (Habakkuk 2:3). You can be gladdened by Christ's presence, because He will come to you at just the right time.

GUARDED BY HIS POWER

We are ready for the fifth anchor of the soul that we find in this miracle. Jesus said to the disciples, "It is I; be not afraid" (John 6:20). Someone has said, "The will of God will never take you where the grace of God cannot keep you." That is everlastingly true.

When He sent the disciples away, Jesus told them to go to the other side of the Sea of Galilee (Matthew 14:22). He did not tell them to go to the middle of the sea and go under. They did not know it, but the disciples were as safe in that storm as they would have been on dry land. Why? Because He would not tell them to go somewhere they couldn't get to and, furthermore, *He was guarding them by His power*.

If I could choose one moment when I would have liked to see Jesus in the flesh, I would choose the moment when He came walking to the disciples on the water. I can just see that kingly form with the wind in His hair as He put His footsteps on the sea, His garments billowing back as He smiled at the storm.

But as Jesus approached them, the disciples began to draw back in terror (Matthew 14:26). They thought they were seeing a ghost. But soon their terror turned to joy as they heard Jesus say, "It is I; be not afraid." Now let me show you something wonderful. What Jesus literally said was, "Don't be afraid, I AM." He was using the name Jehovah, the most sacred name to the Jews.

The Great I AM

At the burning bush, when Moses asked God what name he should give to the people of Israel, God answered, "I AM THAT I AM: and he said, Thus shalt thou say unto the children of Israel, I AM hath sent me unto you" (Exodus 3:13-14). This is the sacred name of God rendered as Jehovah.

Yesterday God is I AM. Today He is I AM. Tomorrow He will be I AM. Jesus was saying to the disciples, "The eternal God, I AM, has come to you. Do not be afraid."

"I AM" is a declaration of power, a proclamation of presence, an announcement of abundance. Jesus is the I AM in the midst of your storm.

Under His Feet

Why did Jesus walk to the disciples on the water? It wasn't just theatrics, I can assure you. It was part of the message of the miracle, the significance of the sign. It was part of something that went beyond the miracle, something for your heart when your friend Trouble comes calling on you.

What was the disciples' biggest problem that day? The stormy water. What was their biggest fear? That they were going to be tossed into that water and feel the waves close over their heads. When Jesus walked on that boiling sea, He was showing them that what they thought was going to be over their heads was already under His feet.

In the same way, whatever may be over your head is under Jesus' feet. Don't ever forget that. Jesus said, "In the world ye shall have tribulation: but be of good cheer; I have overcome the world" (John 16:33).

Indeed He has, and He is now seated in the heavenlies. He is the Head of the church. How could anyone drown with his Head that far above water?

We are overcomers in the Lord Jesus Christ. You may have problems, heartaches, fears, and tears. But you are guarded by His power. He is to you the great I AM. "I am the bread of life. I am the water of life. I am the door. I am the way, the truth, and the life." Jesus is the great I AM in the midst of your storm.

GUIDED BY HIS PURPOSE

Here is the sixth and final anchor of the soul I want to leave with you. *God has not promised you smooth sailing, but He has promised you a safe landing.* You are being guided by His purpose even when your boat is filling up with water.

Let me remind you again that Jesus' purpose for this trip was to get to the other side of the Sea of Galilee. By the time He came walking to the disciples on the sea, however, they were not at all sure they were going to fulfill that purpose. No wonder they "willingly received [Jesus] into the ship" (John 6:21).

Fulfilling God's Purpose

Keep reading and you'll see something amazing: "Immediately the ship was at the land whither they went." There were actually three miracles that occurred here. Jesus not only calmed the storm and suspended the law of gravity to walk on the water, but He also overruled the laws of time and space. In an instant, they were at the other shore.

These men were rowing hard, their backs aching, their brows mingled with perspiration and seawater. But when Jesus came aboard, they reached their destination immediately. God's purpose was fulfilled.

Andrew Murray said, "God is willing to assume the full responsibility for the life totally yielded to Him." No matter how often your friend Trouble may visit you, I can promise you on the authority of God's Word that you are predestined to be like Jesus (Romans 8:29).

God is guiding you toward His purpose. And one of these days, His purpose in you will be fulfilled, for the Bible says, "He which hath begun a good work in you will perform it until the day of Jesus Christ" (Philippians 1:6).

God is going to see you through to His purpose for you. That's a promise. You say, "Adrian, how can you promise that?" I'm not making the promise. I'm simply repeating God's promise. He said, "I will never leave thee, nor forsake thee" (Hebrews 13:5).

God's Forever Purpose

The message of this miracle is that God will see you through. Whatever is over your head is under His feet, so there is nothing too hard for Him. Nothing can thwart His purpose for you. Miracles will cease, but if you go beyond the miracle to Jesus, you will be forever blessed.

One of these days very soon, He is going to step down from the mountain, not by the Sea of Galilee, but from His throne in glory. On that day, walking on water will be like child's play because He will be stepping on the clouds as He comes to us.

The barometer of this world is falling, the winds are whipping up, and the storms are coming. People ask, "What is this world coming to?" This world is coming to Jesus, because Jesus is coming to this world. He is going to step out of heaven with the smile of victory on His face as the great I AM, and the trumpet will sound. Then our little ship will leave the sea of time, and immediately we will be on the shores of eternity.

YOUR RECIPE FOR A MIRACLE

Your Need—God's Peace for Your Despair

God's Supply for Your Need

God has given you His providence to govern you.

- Even when you are sailing into a storm.
- Because you are sailing by Jesus' order.

God has given you His plan to grow you.

- Even when that means growing through trouble.

- Remember the "Breakfast of Champions."

God has given you His prayers to grace you.

- He has a perfect view of your circumstances.
- His eye is on you.

God has given you His presence to gladden you.

- Don't forget He is with you in the storm.
- Even His seeming delays are gracious.

God has given you His power to guard you.

- He is the great I AM.
- What's over your head is under His feet.

God has given you His purpose to guide you.

- Your goal is to fulfill that purpose.
- God's purpose for you is for eternity, not just for today.

How to Meet Your Need in Jesus

- *Resist the temptation to panic in the midst of your storm*: Remember that you are there by God's providential guidance. There is no panic in heaven, only plans.
- *Thank the Lord that He sends storms your way not to sink your boat, not to sink you, but to grow you in your faith.*
- *Praise God that His watchful eye is on you, and that Jesus is praying for you every moment of your trial* (Hebrews 7:25).
- *Draw on the presence of Jesus to gladden your heart in the storm*: Don't fret over what seems to be His delay in coming to you, for when He comes, you have the power of the great I AM with you!
- *Ask God to reveal His purpose for you in your storm*: Then set your heart to fulfill that purpose.

CHAPTER EIGHT

OPENING BLIND EYES

JESUS IS GOD'S LIGHT FOR YOUR DARKNESS

* * *

> For several centuries, down through many dynasties, a village was known for its exquisite and fragile porcelain. Especially striking were its urns: High as tables, wide as chairs, they were admired around the globe for their strong form and delicate beauty. Legend has it that when each urn was finished, there was one final step. The artist broke it—and then put it back together with gold filigree. An ordinary urn was then transformed into a priceless work of art. What seemed finished wasn't . . . until it was broken.[1]

In John 9 we are going to see a miracle that reminds us of those special pieces of porcelain. We are going to see a man whose life was broken by blindness, only to be transformed by the gold filigree of God's grace. This miracle points us to Jesus as God's answer to our darkness. The story begins when Jesus and the disciples meet a man who was blind.

> *And as Jesus passed by, he saw a man which was blind from his birth. And his disciples asked him, saying, Master, who did sin, this man, or his parents, that he was born blind? Jesus answered, Neither hath this man sinned, nor his parents: but that the works of God should be made manifest in him.*
>
> —*John 9:1-3*

Spiritual Blindness Makes Us Beggars

John tells us that this man's problem was physical blindness. But he is also an illustration of a person without the Lord Jesus Christ. Back in John 1:4, the apostle wrote: "In [Jesus] was life; and the life was the light of men." And, "Men loved darkness rather than light because their deeds were evil. For every one that doeth evil hateth the light" (3:19-20).

We Are Blind

What happened when Adam sinned? Adam was suddenly without God in his spirit. He had been made perfect when God created him. He was a temple in which God could live. But God told Adam that in the day he sinned against God, he would surely die (Genesis 2:17). When Adam sinned against God, he did not die physically that day. He lived hundreds of years after that. But Adam died that day spiritually.

What happened was that the spiritual life went out of Adam. John 1:4 says that the "life" of the Lord was "the light of men." So when the Lord went out of Adam, the life went out. And when the life went out, the light went out.

We Are Born Blind

Since that time, every person has been born a child of Adam with the nature of Adam, which means minus God, minus His life, and minus the light. The absence of light brings darkness and blindness. Therefore, this man in John 9 who was born blind is illustrative of every man, woman, boy, and girl who is without the Lord Jesus Christ.

When the Lord went out of Adam, mankind became depraved. When the life went out, mankind became dead. And when the light went out, mankind became darkened. People are all of that when they don't have the Lord.

You don't have to be a vile criminal to be lost. All who are without God are lost. We are all children of Adam, and "in Adam all die" (1 Corinthians 15:22).

So Jesus says to every man and every woman, "You are blind. You cannot see the truth." In John 3:3 Jesus told Nicodemus, "Except a man be born again, he cannot see the kingdom of God." A lost person may have 20/20 eyesight, but he can't understand spiritual things.

Ephesians 4:18 says that those who do not know Christ have had their "understanding darkened, being alienated from the life of God through the ignorance that is in them, because of the blindness of their heart."

There is more than one kind of blindness. There is blindness of the eyes, and there is blindness of the spirit. This man was blind both in his eyes and in his spirit, and he needed Jesus to heal both afflictions.

This man was not only blind, he was born blind. This led the disciples to ask a foolish question, as we read above in verse 2. They assumed that someone had to be at fault for the blind man's condition. Since he was blind from birth, his parents came under suspicion as far as the disciples were concerned.

It is possible, of course, for children to suffer because of their parents' sin. Sometimes babies are born blind because of things like venereal disease, and we know that the children of drug addicts can be born addicted.

But even allowing for the possibility that this man's blindness was the result of sin, the disciples' question was still foolish. How could a baby sin before his birth and be born blind as a result? It sounds like the disciples believed it was possible for a baby to sin in his mother's womb.

Jesus dismissed the silliness of such an idea by declaring them wrong on both counts. Besides, the disciples' question missed the point. The issue was not how this man became blind. The issue was his need for Jesus.

Jesus made it clear that the reason for the man's blindness was to provide an opportunity for God to be glorified in his life. In other words, the disciples wanted to look back and focus on history. Jesus pointed them ahead to the glory of God that was about to be made manifest in this man's life.

So here we have a man who illustrates the spiritual condition of all mankind. He was blind. More than that, he was born blind.

We are all born blind spiritually. The Bible says, "I was shapen in iniquity; and in sin did my mother conceive me" (Psalm 51:5). David was not saying he was conceived out of wedlock. He was confessing that he was conceived with a sinful nature and was born a sinner.

Even the most precious child you can imagine has a sinful nature and needs to be saved. In Ephesians 2:3 Paul tells believers that when they were lost, they were "by nature the children of wrath, even as others."

We Are Beggars

Not only was this man in John 9 born blind, but his blindness had reduced him to begging. "The neighbors therefore, and they which before had seen him that was blind, said, Is not this he that sat and begged?" (v. 8).

God designed us to be kings, to rule over His creation. When God created Adam and Eve and placed them in the Garden of Eden, He told them to "subdue" the earth and "have dominion" over every part of His creation (Genesis 1:28).

Adam and Eve were to rule as king and queen of Planet Earth. But mankind, though created to be spiritual royalty, has been reduced to being a blind beggar because of sin.

Someone may say, "I'm not a beggar. I have a lot of money salted away. I may have been born blind spiritually, but I'm certainly no beggar." But that person does not understand the kind of poverty the Bible is talking about.

Remember what the risen Jesus said to the wealthy church at Laodicea? "Thou sayest, I am rich, and increased with goods, and have need of nothing; and knowest not that thou art wretched, and miserable, and *poor*, and *blind*, and *naked*" (Revelation 3:17, emphasis added). What a telling picture of mankind without the Lord Jesus Christ!

THE BLIND NEED MORE THAN LIGHT

Here's a second truth I want you to understand: the blind need more than light in order to see. This blind man was in the very presence of Jesus, "the light of the world" (v. 5). But he still could not see.

The Blind Need Sight

A blind person would be foolish to deny the presence of light simply because he cannot see it. John 9 tells us that blind people need more than light to see; they need *sight*. There's a great truth here. There can be no sight without light, but no light can be seen without sight.

I have been deep in the famous Carlsbad Caverns in New Mexico when they turn out all the lights. The darkness is so deep, you can almost slice it. Even if you have 20/20 vision, you can't see a thing because there is no sight without light. No one can be saved apart from Jesus, the light of the world.

But conversely, there can be light without sight. A blind person can stand in the hot sun at high noon and still deny the presence of light. People can be standing in the presence of Jesus and yet deny His light.

This is important to understand when it comes to reaching the lost. It's not enough just to shine the light of the Gospel upon people. Unless God the Holy Spirit opens their blinded eyes, they will not see. Paul said:

> *If our gospel be hid, it is hid to them that are lost: in whom the god of this world hath blinded the minds of them which believe*

not, lest the light of the glorious gospel of Christ, who is the image of God, should shine unto them.

—2 Corinthians 4:3-4

Satan cannot put out the light of Christ. So what does he do? He blinds the heart and mind of the unbelieving. This is why it takes more than preaching to get people saved.

As a young preacher I used to think that all you had to do to get people saved was to tell them how to be saved. Just turn on the light. But it doesn't matter how much light is present if the person is blind. He can't see it.

It takes more than light to save someone. It takes sight, and only God can make the spiritually blind see. It takes more than preaching or witnessing to get people saved. I can preach the truth, and you can share the truth, but only the Holy Spirit can *impart* truth.

Those who witness must have the anointing of the Holy Spirit, because we are dependent upon God to open blinded eyes to the Gospel of Jesus Christ. We need to understand that nobody can be argued or educated into the kingdom of heaven.

Now don't misunderstand me. We must let the light shine. We must preach and share the truth. But we need to remember that there is another dimension to this business of salvation. The meaning of this miracle is not only that Jesus is the light of the world, but that only God can open blinded eyes. So again, we see the need to *go beyond the miracle to Jesus.*

A brilliant high school student once wrote to the newspaper in our city. He ridiculed Christianity and even belief in God. He summed up his letter with these words: "When men stop believing in a non-existent God to save them from a non-existent hell, then the world will once again be populated by men rather than sheep."

Later this young man came to our church to jeer and pick an argument. But the finger of God touched him, and he came to Christ. Later still, I had a conversation with him, during which he said an amazing thing. "Pastor Rogers, before I surrendered my will, I was so sure that God did not exist. Now I can't even remember the arguments."

Indeed, it was not a counterargument but God Himself who opened this young man's eyes.

The Blind Need Jesus

Notice that when Jesus prepared to heal the blind man, He did something unusual and remarkable.

> *When he had thus spoken [He had just said, "I am the light of the world"], he spat on the ground, and made clay of the spittle, and he anointed the eyes of the blind man with the clay, and said unto him, Go, wash in the pool of Siloam, (which is by interpretation, Sent.) He went his way therefore, and washed, and came seeing.*
>
> —*vv. 6-7*

Why did Jesus do that? What does the clay represent? I believe it represents the same thing that those clay waterpots represented in the miracle of the water turned to wine (John 2:6).

God made man from the dust of the earth (Genesis 2:7). Because clay speaks of humanity, it speaks of our weakness, failure, and spiritual inability. When Jesus put clay on this man's eyes, the clay actually sealed out the light even further. This action symbolized what was wrong with him—that is, his lost humanity, his blinded spiritual nature.

But Jesus did not leave the clay on his eyes. He told him to go wash it off in a pool whose name meant "Sent." Why did the Holy Spirit put this into the text? What is the significance of having the man wash in a pool called Sent?

In John 8:12 Jesus said, "I am the light of the world: he that followeth me shall not walk in darkness, but shall have the light of life." But the Jews, particularly the scribes and Pharisees, would not accept Jesus' testimony concerning Himself. So Jesus said to them in verse 23, "Ye are from beneath; I am from above: ye are of this world; I am not of this world."

Jesus was saying, "I am from heaven. My origin is heaven." He was speaking of His identification with God the Father. Verse 26 of John 8 says, "He that sent me is true." Jesus said again in verse 29, "He that sent me is with me." In other words, Jesus is the "Sent One" from the heavenly Father. Then we come to John 9:4, where Jesus said before He healed this man, "I must work the works of him that sent me." Finally, He instructs the blind man to go and wash in a pool called Sent.

Do you see the progression? Jesus is saying that this pool represented Him. He is the "Sent One" from heaven. He is heaven's answer to our darkness.

The dust and dirt of our sinful humanity block out the light. But Jesus has been sent from above to wash away the dirt of sin and restore spiritual sight. The blind need more than light to see.

They need sight, and Jesus Christ is the only One who can give them that sight.

Opened Eyes Must Learn to See

A third truth we need to learn from this miracle is that in the spiritual realm newly opened eyes must learn to see. This man in John 9 is no longer blind. Jesus has given him sight. Now he must learn who Jesus is.

Adjusting to the Light

Notice how this man progresses in his spiritual understanding. After he was healed, the people who knew him asked, "How were thine eyes opened?" (v. 10).

A man. He answered them in verse 11: "A man that is called Jesus made clay . . . and I received sight." At this point, the Healer was just a man named Jesus. That's all the healed man knew about Him.

They then brought him to the Pharisees, because the miracle had taken place on the Sabbath. Now the interrogation really began, because the Pharisees hated Jesus and wanted to discredit Him.

A prophet. Some accused Jesus of being "a sinner" (v. 16). So they asked the man for his opinion. "He is a prophet" (v. 17). The healed man was beginning to think about all this, and it dawned on him that anyone who could do what Jesus did had to be more than a man. He must have been a prophet.

That answer got the Pharisees stirred up, so now they really began to badger him. They tried again to get him to denounce Jesus as a sinner (v. 24).

I love his answer in verse 25: "Whether he be a sinner or no, I know not: one thing I know, that, whereas I was blind, now I see."

A man sent from God. That sparked an angry outburst from the Pharisees (v. 28), and this man then proceeded to give them a remarkable lecture in theology (vv. 30-33). He called Jesus "a worshipper of God [who] doeth his will" (v. 31). Then he confessed, "If this man were not of God, he could do nothing" (v. 33).

You can see this man's spiritual eyes steadily adjusting to the "light" of Jesus Christ. First Jesus is a man, then a prophet, then a man sent from God. He was getting the message of the miracle! Jesus was sent from God to open blind eyes, and this man began to realize that this is what had happened to him.

Enabled to Believe

The man's reward for testifying to Jesus was to be "cast . . . out" (v. 34), which means the Pharisees excommunicated him from worshiping at the temple. Jesus is the light of the world, but the Pharisees were the blight of the world. Religion without Jesus is a spiritual pestilence.

The Pharisees shut this man out, but Jesus sought him out. The man's eyes were open, but he was not yet saved. Jesus enabled him to believe by giving him understanding. Jesus was leading him from a non-saving faith to a saving faith. The man was growing in his understanding about Jesus until he came to actually trust Jesus Christ with his very soul.

This man illustrates that it takes more than light to see spiritually. It takes sight. And he reminds us that once you get both light and sight, you still have to learn to see.

From Ignorance to Faith

This man began with honest ignorance. Humorist Will Rogers once said that a man doesn't show his ignorance by not knowing so much but by knowing so much that ain't so. This man only knew what he knew. "Whereas I was blind, now I see." He wasn't afraid to say, "I don't know" when the Pharisees asked him a question to which he did not have the answer.

This is a good lesson for us. Don't be afraid to give your testimony for fear that someone will ask you something you don't know. If anybody does that, just say, "I don't know." When you are honest enough to admit what you don't know, people will believe you when you tell them what you do know.

This man told what he knew. He was the recipient of a miracle, and no one could argue with that. He started with what I call honest ignorance about the person of Jesus.

But Jesus did not leave him in ignorance. The Bible says the Holy Spirit guides us into truth. The Holy Spirit does not give us truth already packaged and pre-digested. Learning the truth is a process. Once you have the light, you must still learn to see.

The man of John 9 went through a progression from ignorance to faith. He had encountered religion at its worst; so now he was ready for the final ray of light that helped his opened eyes to see. Notice how his faith ripens:

> *Jesus heard that they had cast him out; and when he had found him, he said unto him, Dost thou believe on the Son of God? He answered and said, Who is he, Lord, that I might believe on him? And Jesus said unto him, Thou hast both seen him, and it is he that talketh with thee. And he said, Lord, I believe. And he worshipped him.*
>
> —*vv.* 35-38

This man who had been given his sight was learning to see. This is the way people come to the Lord Jesus Christ. God has to open their eyes. The Holy Spirit has to give them spiritual sight. But then they must learn to see, to grow in knowledge until they come to full-orbed faith.

Handling Spiritual Truth

Jesus said, "Take heed therefore how ye hear: for whosoever hath, to him shall be given; and whosoever hath not, from him shall be taken even that which he seemeth to have" (Luke 8:18).

Jesus is telling us to be careful how we respond to spiritual truth. If you have a desire for truth, you'll be given more truth. But if you don't have a desire for truth, even that which you seem to have will be taken away from you.

In Romans 1:17 Paul says, "Therein is the righteousness of God revealed from faith to faith: as it is written, The just shall live by faith." How does God speak to you? "From faith to faith."

When this man acknowledged that Jesus opened his eyes, that was a little bit of faith. When he said Jesus was a prophet, he went to another level of faith. Then he said Jesus was sent from

God. And finally he worshiped Jesus as the Son of God; he believed in Jesus and was saved. He went "from faith to faith."

Proverbs 4:18 tells us, "The path of the just is as the shining light, that shineth more and more unto the perfect day." At first, we see a gray dawn. Then the sun comes over the horizon, and we can see a little better. But there are still shadows with very little color.

Then the sun rises a little bit more, and we can see better still, but the shadows are long. Then finally it is high noon, and there are no shadows. That's the way God gives us spiritual wisdom. We go from darkness to shadows to the full blaze of the knowledge of God.

We Must Admit Our Blindness

If it's true that we are blind beggars from birth who need both light and spiritual sight to see the truth about God, there is only one conclusion we can draw. Our greatest need is to confess and admit our spiritual blindness, our need of Christ. Denial is deadly, but acknowledgment of need accompanied by trust in Him brings life.

Let's go back to the final verses of John 9:

> *And Jesus said, For judgment I am come into this world, that they which see not might see; and that they which see might be made blind. And some of the Pharisees which were with him heard these words, and said unto him, Are we blind also? Jesus said unto them, If ye were blind, ye should have no sin: but now ye say, We see; therefore your sin remaineth.*
>
> —*vv. 39-41*

Rejecting the Light

You've undoubtedly heard the old saying, "There are none so blind as those who will not see." Those who like the Pharisees claimed they had no blindness, Jesus sent away blind. Those who claimed to be full, Jesus sent away empty. Those who claimed to be righteous, He sent away unforgiven.

Man's greatest need is to admit his spiritual blindness. Just as light obeyed increases light, so light refused increases darkness. Paul says of those who refuse to repent of their sin, "When they knew God, they glorified him not as God, neither were thankful; but became vain in their imaginations, and their foolish heart was darkened" (Romans 1:21).

There can be no greater sin than to reject the light of Jesus Christ. Once a man hears the Gospel and his heart opens to the Word of God, if he does not act upon that light and go from faith to faith until he believes in Jesus Christ, his condemnation is doubled.

Why? Because he is not only judged for the disease, but he is judged because he refused the cure. Listen to Jesus:

> *This is the condemnation, that light is come into the world, and men loved darkness rather than light, because their deeds were evil. For every one that doeth evil hateth the light, neither cometh to the light, lest his deeds should be reproved.*
>
> —*John 3:19-20*

When God comes to judge the world, He is not going to judge the world primarily because of the sin that was committed, but because of the light that was rejected.

THE LIGHT OF THE WORLD

Here is the message of this miracle: *we must come to Jesus, who is the light of the world* (John 9:5). Jesus alone can cure our spiritual blindness. Because of sin, we are born as blind beggars. But our blind eyes can be opened by the grace of God. The human mind can be opened and the heart quickened to understand the Gospel of Jesus Christ.

Once our eyes open up to the light, we must live up to the light we have. We must walk in the light. We must follow the light, going beyond the miracle to Jesus Himself. *Believe in the miracle, but trust in Jesus!*

YOUR RECIPE FOR A MIRACLE

Your Need—God's Light for Your Darkness

Spiritual blindness makes us beggars.

- We are blind.
- We are born blind.
- We are beggars.

As spiritually blind people, we need more than light.

- We need spiritual sight.
- We need Jesus.

Eyes that are opened by Jesus must learn to see.

- We must adjust to the light.
- We must be enabled to believe.
- We must move from ignorance to faith.
- We must learn how to handle spiritual truth.

We must admit our blindness.

- We dare not reject the light.
- We must see Jesus as the light of the world.

God's Supply for Your Need

- Light for our blinded eyes and heart.
- Spiritual riches for the poverty that makes us beggars.
- Spiritual sight for our opened eyes.
- Jesus is the Light of the world!

How to Meet Your Need in Jesus

• *Test your spiritual eyesight to determine whether you have opened your eyes and heart to the Lord Jesus*: If you have any doubt about your relationship with Christ, don't rest until you have settled the issue.

• *If you have already trusted Christ as your Savior, spend time thanking Him for the spiritual riches you have in Christ*: Read passages such as Ephesians 1:3-14 and Colossians 2:13-15 to refresh your memory of what God has done for you in Christ. Then share the blessing with your family or a friend.

• Read 1 Corinthians 2:9-16 and *thank God for the wonderful gift of the Holy Spirit's illumination of your heart and mind*, which allows your opened eyes to see and understand the truth of God.

• *Praise God that He sent Jesus to this earth to open the eyes of the blind*: Rejoice that Jesus saw fit to open your eyes to the truth about Himself. Step outside into the light and offer a prayer of thanks for Jesus, the Light of the world!

CHAPTER NINE

RAISING LAZARUS

JESUS IS GOD'S LIFE FOR YOUR DEATH

* * *

He was young, tall, and sun-crowned. He was a neighboring pastor whose name was Bob. He said to me, "Adrian, there is an old man who is about to die. I don't believe he knows about the Lord Jesus Christ. Would you visit him and share Jesus?"

"Sure, I will," I answered.

When I called on the old man, I didn't beat around the bush. "Hello, I'm Adrian Rogers," I said. "I wonder if I might come in and talk with you a while about the Lord Jesus and how you can know Him personally and go to heaven."

"Come in," he replied. In a short time the old man humbly bowed his head, prayed, and received Christ and the gift of eternal life.

That is a wonderful story, but it doesn't end there. A few days later my friend Bob, the young pastor who was seemingly so full of health and vitality, was having lunch with his wife. After the meal, Bob started across the living room of his home. Then he gave a gasp and fell dead on the living room floor.

He had said to me that the old man had only a few days to live. The old man lived for years. It was the young preacher who had only days to live.

The fact of death is certain. The time of death is uncertain. Man is the only creature who knows he is going to die and is desperately trying to forget it. Mention death, and people will change the subject more quickly than they change the television channel.

SOME VIEWS OF LIFE

Not only does man fear death, he really does not enjoy life. Consider some of the views of life from people famous and unknown, from past eras and today.

Nineteenth-century British leader Benjamin Disraeli said, "Youth is a blunder, manhood a struggle, old age a regret."

William Shakespeare said, "Life is a tale told by an idiot, full of sound and fury, signifying nothing."

According to writer George Santayana, "Life is not a spectacle or a feast; it is a predicament."

Samuel Butler said, "Life is one long process of getting tired."

The French say, "Life is an onion. One cries while peeling it."

Some college students were asked to give a definition of life for the school newspaper, and here are some definitions that won honorable mention. One student said, "Life is a joke that isn't even funny." Another wrote, "Life is a disease, for which the only cure is death." A third student offered this opinion: "Life is a jail sentence that we get for the crime of being born."

Then there is the life philosophy of "Dr. Death" himself, the infamous Dr. Jack Kevorkian. He recently expounded on his view of life by saying, when asked about religion and faith, "People like us base their whole outlook on mythology. I have my own god, Johann Sebastian Bach." Then he said, "Why not? You invent gods. At least he's not invented."

Let me give you one more view of life. Jesus Christ said in John 10:10, "I am come that they might have life, and that they might have it more abundantly."

Who gets your vote for a healthy view of life—"Dr. Death" or the Lord of life? I'll go with the Lord of life!

So many people today don't have life—they only have existence. They are fighting to live while they're living to fight. They are just drawing their breath and their salary, and one day monotonously turns into another. They exist, but they are not living!

These people have got things all backwards. When you take the word *live* and turn it backwards, it spells *evil*. That pretty well sums up life without Jesus. A life *lived* without Jesus, a life lived backwards, gives you *devil*.

Jesus has come that you might have life and have it abundantly. Satan is a thief who comes to rob you of life, to steal, kill, and destroy (John 10:10). A person is foolish if he does not decide to live for the Lord Jesus Christ.

GOD'S ANSWER TO DEATH

The seventh miracle with a message, the final sign with a significance, we are going to consider from the Gospel of John is an appropriate capstone to our study because it deals with the ultimate issues of life and death. It is the miracle of the raising of Lazarus, and the message it holds for us is perhaps the most wonderful of all: *Jesus is God's answer to man's death!*

This miracle is recorded in John 11, a moving and triumphant chapter in which we see Jesus displaying His power over death. John 11 is one of the longest chapters in the New Testament. A verse-by-verse study is outside our purposes here, so I will summarize the setting and some other details so we can examine the miracle and its meaning.

We know from the early verses of this great chapter that Jesus was notified of the illness of Lazarus, His beloved friend from Bethany, the brother of Mary and Martha (vv. 1-3).

Even though Lazarus eventually died, Jesus delayed going to Bethany (vv. 4-16). He did so because His primary concern was "the glory of God, that the Son of God might be glorified thereby" (v. 4). He was fully aware of the miracle He was going to perform.

When Jesus and the disciples finally arrived in Bethany, we come to that famous scene in which Martha went out to meet Him. I want to pick up the narrative at this point.

> *Then said Martha unto Jesus, Lord, if thou hadst been here, my brother had not died. But I know, that even now, whatsoever thou wilt ask of God, God will give it thee. . . . Jesus said unto her, I am the resurrection, and the life: he that believeth in me, though he were dead, yet shall he live: and whosoever liveth and believeth in me shall never die.*
>
> *—vv. 21-22, 25-26*

Here is the message in the miracle. Jesus put it right on the line before He even raised Lazarus from the dead: "I am the resurrection, and the life." Jesus is the answer to the problem of death. This is why I will repeat again: *believe in the miracle, but trust in Jesus.*

The raising of Lazarus actually happened. We can believe it. But our faith does not rest in this historical miracle. Our faith must be in the Lord of the miracle, Jesus Christ.

Let me give you three lessons you must accept if you would glean what God wants you to learn from this wonderful miracle. If you want the full, abundant life Jesus promised, you must take three important steps.

EXPERIENCE LIFE IN JESUS

The first step you need to take to have abundant life is to experience life in Jesus.

Look back at John 11:14, where Jesus said plainly, "Lazarus is dead." That was all that could be said about this man who was Jesus' beloved friend.

You see, Lazarus had a king-sized problem. It did not matter that Lazarus may have had a full head of hair or a lean body. It did not matter that he may have been well dressed. It did not even matter that Lazarus was surrounded by two loving sisters and a host of friends.

No matter how many things might have been right about Lazarus, there was nothing really right about him because there was one huge thing that was very wrong about him. He was dead.

The Living Dead

Spiritually, Lazarus represents a multitude of people we come in contact with every day. They may have many wonderful qualities, and they may look sharp. But if they do not know the Lord Jesus Christ personally as Savior, they are as spiritually dead as Lazarus was physically dead.

Anyone who has not received life from Jesus is dead in trespasses and sins (Ephesians 2:1; compare 1 Timothy 5:6). Do you know any people who are dead even while they live? The city of Memphis, where I serve as pastor, is full of them. So is your city or town.

Those Who Cannot Die

The opposite of people who are dead while they live is people we call dead but who are not dead at all. These are people who know Jesus and have transferred their residence from earth to heaven.

If your mother and father knew Jesus but are no longer with you, they are not dead. They're kicking up gold dust on the streets of heaven!

It is impossible for those who know the Lord to die. If you are a believer in Jesus Christ and you want to meet a person who cannot die, take a look in the mirror!

You say, "Now wait a minute, Adrian. We're all going to die." Wrong! It's absolutely, totally impossible for a bona fide believer in Jesus Christ to die. I didn't say that—Jesus did. "Whosoever liveth and believeth in me shall never die" (John 11:26).

What we call death occurs when our bodies cease to function.

Paul describes this when he writes, "If our earthly house of this tabernacle were dissolved . . ." (2 Corinthians 5:1). He then contrasts our earthly bodies with our eternal, resurrection bodies.

Yes, my "earthly house" may decay someday. It may drop into the grave. But I like what Dwight L. Moody used to say: "Someday you will hear that Moody is dead. Don't you believe it. I'll be more alive than I ever was."

So if you ever hear that Adrian Rogers is dead, don't believe it! Whose word are you going to take—a doctor's or Jesus'?

You see, I cannot die. I will just move out of my temporary "tent" (that's the meaning of the word "tabernacle") into my glorified body. "To be absent from the body [is] to be present with the Lord" (2 Corinthians 5:8). We never really die when we know the Lord Jesus Christ.

One of the most unusual people I ever had the joy of knowing was a man named Charlie Fisher. He was a little wiry guy whom we used to call "Uncle Charlie." I believe he was more on fire for Jesus than any man I've ever known.

Uncle Charlie was a member of the church I used to pastor in Ft. Pierce, Florida. He had an old, canvas-covered airplane that he would use for a very unusual form of witnessing. He would fly over county fairs and dump out bushels of tracts.

Then Uncle Charlie would fly back over the place with a loudspeaker and preach to the people on the ground, telling them about the Lord Jesus. He would also conduct street meetings and do all kinds of strange things to spread the faith.

I could tell you many stories about Uncle Charlie Fisher. But I think the strangest thing Uncle Charlie ever did was preach his own funeral.

What Uncle Charlie did was to tell his son, "When I die, just gather my friends around for the funeral. You don't have to do anything. Just gather my friends. I've recorded my message, and all you have to do is push the play button." And that's exactly what happened! Charlie Fisher preached his own funeral!

When the day came, all of Charlie's friends were there. Uncle Charlie's body was there, but he wasn't. Someone pushed the button on the tape recorder, and the people heard, "Hello, friends, this is Charlie Fisher. I'm up here in heaven, and it is wonderful."

Then Charlie proceeded to tell all about heaven and how wonderful it was. Then he said, "I want all of you down there to come and meet me in heaven."

I'll admit, that is a very unusual example of someone who "being dead yet speaketh" (Hebrews 11:4). But I warned you, Charlie Fisher was an unusual man!

However, what Charlie did is a good illustration of what we are talking about here. When he spoke at his own funeral, he was indeed alive. The Bible says that the person who lives in pleasure is dead even though he or she is alive (1 Timothy 5:6). But the person who believes in Jesus has everlasting life.

The Universal Need for New Life

The Gospels record that Jesus raised three people from the dead. The first was the daughter of Jairus, a little girl who was sick at home and had died by the time Jesus arrived. But He raised her from the dead (Mark 5:21-43).

The second person Jesus raised from the dead was a young

man from Nain (Luke 7:11-17). Jesus met the funeral procession carrying this young man to his grave and broke up the procession by raising him from the dead.

The third person Jesus raised was Lazarus. The little girl had just been dead a few hours or so, and the young man had not yet been buried. So in each case there was no decay. But Lazarus had been dead for four days by the time Jesus raised him. Decay had certainly set in.

But let me ask you a question: which of these three people was the most dead? Obviously, they were equally dead. There's no such thing as being a little bit dead or being more dead than some other deceased person. Dead is dead.

My point is this: sometimes we see people who have wallowed in the filth of sin, whose bodies are covered with the scars and the stench of iniquity. We turn up our noses and say, "My, look at that."

But you need to understand that a man sitting in church, all dressed up and looking great, is just as dead as the guy in the gutter if he does not have Jesus. Dead is dead.

The man in church may never have touched drink or drugs, but without Jesus Christ he is dead in his trespasses and sins. All of us need to experience life in Christ.

How to Experience Life in Christ

How does a person experience real life? If we were to listen to the various social engineers around us today in the academic, professional, and political worlds, we would conclude that what people need today is the four E's: example, encouragement, environment, and education. Our nation is spending billions of dollars on programs to implement these ideas. Let's see how far they get us.

We are talking about how to experience life in Christ, about bringing dead people back to life. So let's suppose we had a dead man we were trying to bring back to life. How are we going to raise him from the dead?

How about by example? Would it do any good to bring someone in and say, "I have a dead person here who needs to know how to live. So show him how a person acts when he is alive. Do fifty push-ups or something. Show him what it means to be alive." Do you think a living person's example is going to raise a dead man? No, that won't do it.

So let's try encouragement. Bring in the best motivational speaker you can find. Line up a squad of cheerleaders. Even get all the pastors together to cheer the dead man on. "Come on, you can do it. Get up and walk."

Sounds silly, doesn't it? You can't encourage a dead man back to life. How about changing his environment? Maybe that's the answer. Suppose we take that dead man and put him in a room full of living people. Just get him in the right environment—that will give him life, won't it? No way.

Environment is not the answer, but there are people in this world who never seem to learn that. I would remind you that Adam and Eve got in trouble in the only perfect environment earth has ever known, the Garden of Eden. You couldn't have a better environment than that. Environment is not the answer.

Let's try the fourth E, education. Maybe that dead man just doesn't understand the difference between life and death. Get him a medical book, and we'll educate him. We'll show him what life involves and how the body is supposed to function. Then he will know how to live, and he will come back to life. Absurd.

The four E's are not the answer. A dead person needs life from the Lord Jesus Christ. That's why Jesus raised Lazarus from the grave, to show us this revolutionary truth. I want to return to the narrative in John 11 and see how Jesus raised Lazarus from the dead.

After Mary had run out to meet Jesus and express her grief, He asked to be shown where Lazarus was buried (vv. 28-34). Then we have the brief but remarkable note that "Jesus wept," even knowing He was there to raise Lazarus.

When Jesus arrived at the grave, He said, "Take ye away the stone" (v. 39). He reassured Martha of His promise and offered a prayer of simple trust and confidence to the Father (vv. 40-42). Then He gave the command in a loud voice, "Lazarus, come forth" (v. 43). No pleading, no argument, no doubt. Just a word from the Lord, and Lazarus came out of the grave.

How do you experience life in Christ? The same way Lazarus experienced new life—by the Word of God. Jesus said in John 6:63, "It is the spirit that quickeneth; the flesh profiteth nothing: the words that I speak unto you, they are spirit, and they are life."

We are born again by the Word of God, which is "quick, and powerful" (Hebrews 4:12). The word "quick" means "alive," energized with power.

How do you raise a dead person? By the Word of God. That's the reason Paul tells us we should be "holding forth the word of life" to others (Philippians 2:16). It is the Word that gives life.

EXERCISE LIBERTY THROUGH JESUS

I spent a lot of time on the first point because it is so foundational to everything else in the Christian life and so crucial to the message of this miracle. If you don't have life in Jesus, nothing else we are going to talk about is possible.

But once we have experienced life in Jesus, we must exercise liberty through Jesus. Notice that when Lazarus came out of the grave, he was still tied up hand and foot in his graveclothes. Jesus said, "Loose him, and let him go" (v. 44).

Can you imagine that scene? Lazarus comes hobbling out of the open mouth of that cave. He has life, but he doesn't have liberty. He's bound and gagged. He can't walk, he can't work, he can't speak, he can't see. He has life, but he needs to be set free.

Lazarus at this stage of the miracle was like so many people today—saved, but not living in victory. They have been to Calvary for pardon, but they've not yet been to Pentecost for power. Somehow they have bogged down between Calvary and Pentecost. They have life, but they don't have liberty.

You would not have wanted to invite Lazarus to dinner at this particular stage in his resurrection. He had life, but he was still bound in stinking graveclothes. The stench of death was still upon him. He needed to be set free from the old life.

Jesus did not simply come to give you life. He came to give you *abundant* life. He doesn't want you wearing the graveclothes of the old ways.

"Ye shall know the truth, and the truth shall make you free," Jesus said in John 8:32. In verse 36 of that chapter He said, "If the Son therefore shall make you free, ye shall be free indeed." Many believers are still bound by the old loves, the old lusts, the old learning, and the old lies. We are to put off "the old man" (Ephesians 4:22; Colossians 3:9)—to renounce him and walk in newness of life.

The ministry of the church is twofold: to call forth the dead and to unwrap the saints—to give them liberty. I thank God for those who unwrapped me!

ENJOY LOVE FOR JESUS

A third truth from the miracle of the raising of Lazarus is evident in John 12:1-2:

> *Then Jesus six days before the Passover came to Bethany, where Lazarus was which had been dead, whom he raised from the dead. There they made him a supper; and Martha served: but Lazarus was one of them that sat at the table with him.*

Don't you like that? The one who has been given new life by Jesus and was set at liberty by Jesus is now fellowshiping with Jesus. Lazarus has gone from the tomb to the table. There he is, face to face with Jesus, enjoying a meal with Him.

Wouldn't you love to have that kind of intimate fellowship with Jesus? You can, whenever you commune with Him and walk with Him, and in a special way every time you come to the Lord's Table—a meal with the Lord Jesus Christ.

Jesus seeks fellowship with His people. He said in Revelation 3:20, "Behold, I stand at the door, and knock: if any man hear my voice, and open the door, I will come in to him, and will sup with him, and he with me."

We read many times in the Gospels that Jesus invited His disciples to eat with Him. He would say, "Come and dine." Some people say we Christians put too much emphasis on eating together. Maybe we don't do it enough!

It is our legacy to fellowship with Jesus and with one another. Here was Lazarus, sitting at the table in his own house with the Lord Jesus. I wish I could have listened to that conversation.

Living for Christ is not a penalty you pay in order to get to heaven. I'd want to be a Christian even if there were no heaven. Just to know the Lord Jesus Christ, to love Him and fellowship with Him and to know His love and fellowship for and with me, is worth it all.

Express Loyalty to Jesus

As His followers, we ought to express loyalty to Jesus. Look again at John 12:

> *Much people of the Jews therefore knew that [Lazarus] was there: and they came not for Jesus' sake only, but that they might see Lazarus also, whom he had raised from the dead. But the chief priests consulted that they might put Lazarus also to death; because that by reason of him many of the Jews went away, and believed on Jesus.*
>
> —*vv. 9-11*

The man who had been given life and liberty by Jesus loved Jesus and expressed loyalty to Jesus. Lazarus was standing up for Jesus, testifying about Him. That made him dangerous to Satan's kingdom. Many of the Jews believed in Christ because of Lazarus. People were coming to Jesus and getting saved.

This rankled the chief priests and the Pharisees, in whom the milk of human kindness had curdled. They got together and said, "We've got to do something about this man Lazarus. He's turning everyone to Jesus. We need to shut him up. He's a threat—let's put him to death."

What irony! They wanted to kill Lazarus, the man who had already been to the grave once. Do you think Lazarus was worried about their plan? Do you think death held any more terrors for this man?

I don't think he was intimidated at all by the fact that they wanted to put him to death. Satan is the sinister minister of fear, and the Bible says that through the fear of death he keeps people in bondage (Hebrews 2:15).

But Lazarus was no longer afraid of death. He already knew he served the Lord of Life. He already knew that if they destroyed his body, all they would do was hasten him on to heaven. So he gave bold testimony about Jesus.

We are not ready to live until we are no longer afraid to die. And when we are no longer afraid to die, then we can live as Lazarus lived. When we have life and liberty and love and fellowship with Jesus and are ready to express our loyalty to Him, we will know the abundant life Jesus promised to give us.

The Answer to Your Problem

The bottom line is: *if Jesus can raise Lazarus from the dead, He can deal with any problem you and I will ever have.*

Many people ask, "What is the answer to my dilemma?" The answer to your difficulty is not *what*, it's *who*. The answer to your problem—any problem—is Jesus.

The greatest predicament anyone will ever have is that he is spiritually dead, without life. There is no obstacle more insurmountable than death. But Jesus can bring life out of death. Jesus can give you eternal life. Believe in Him, and you will never die.

Think again of the story of the four men who brought a paralyzed man to Jesus on a stretcher (Mark 2:1-12). Picture these four men telling their paralyzed friend that they are going to carry him to Jesus. But he says, "Jesus can't do anything for me. I am totally paralyzed."

So one of the four men says, "Well, I was blind, but Jesus opened my eyes, and now I can see."

But the paralyzed man says, "That was just your eyes. I'm paralyzed all over."

The man carrying another corner of the stretcher says, "Wait a minute. Let me tell you about my withered arm. Jesus straightened and healed my arm."

The paralyzed man objects again. "That was just an arm. My entire body is paralyzed."

The third man says, "I was deaf, but Jesus opened my ears." The paralyzed man is still not convinced. After all, opening ears is not as hard as healing a paralyzed body.

Imagine the man carrying the fourth corner of the stretcher saying, "Healing a paralyzed body is no problem for Jesus. I know that because my name is Lazarus, and I was dead."

End of discussion.

I don't care what situation or crisis you face—the One who can raise the dead is the answer. No problem is too big for Him. That's the reason I believe this miracle occurs last in John's succession of miracles with a message—signs with a significance.

Again, *believe in miracles, but trust in Jesus.* He did not come merely to open blind eyes, unstop deaf ears, or straighten withered arms. He did not even come to raise people temporarily from the grave. He came to save us from our sins, so that we might have life and have it more abundantly.

YOUR RECIPE FOR A MIRACLE

Your Need: God's Life for Your Death

Those without Christ can be called the living dead.

- Without Christ, we are spiritually dead (Ephesians 2:1).
- Without Christ, life becomes mere existence.

Every person needs new life in Christ.

- The fact of death is certain.
- Only Jesus can give eternal life in place of death (John 11:25-26).

God's Supply for Your Need

- He wants you to experience abundant life *in* Jesus (John 10:10).
- He wants you to exercise spiritual liberty *through* Jesus.
- He wants you to experience and enjoy love *for* Jesus.
- He wants you to express your loyalty *to* Jesus.

How to Meet Your Need in Jesus

• *Read John 10:10, and claim Jesus' promise of abundant life for you*: Ask Him to reveal and remove anything in your life that Satan may be using to rob you of the joy of eternal life.

• *Ask God to set you free from any habit, thinking pattern, or besetting sin that may have you spiritually bound and unable to experience the liberty Jesus has for you* (John 8:36).

• *Deepen your love for Jesus by spending time with Him in prayer and in His Word on a daily basis*: Remember that Jesus desires intimate fellowship with you and is in fact seeking such fellowship (Revelation 3:20).

• *Express your loyalty to Jesus* by telling someone else about Him, standing up for Him in your home, at work, and in your neighborhood, and doing all you can to bring others to know Him.

CHAPTER TEN

THE MAXIMUM MIRACLE

* * *

What is the most stupendous miracle the human mind can envision? Perhaps to raise the dead? Actually, there is an even greater miracle than that—the miracle of the new birth.

I am not saying that as a cop-out. I am not trying to excuse myself or any of us from failing to experience dramatic miracles.

Remember that John's purpose for recounting the seven miracles in his Gospel is to bring us to Jesus and the abundant life He alone can give us through the new birth. Listen again to what the apostle writes:

> *And many other signs truly did Jesus in the presence of his disciples, which are not written in this book: but these are written, that ye might believe that Jesus is the Christ, the Son of God; and that believing ye might have life through his name.*
>
> —*John 20:30-31*

A Man with Miracles on His Mind

The maximum miracle is seen in the life of Nicodemus, a leading citizen of New Testament times. He was a ruler of the Jews, gifted and respected. His very name means "superior." Yet he was strongly impressed with the miracles done by Jesus.

Nicodemus was driven to know more about this miracle-worker, so much so that he came to Jesus at nighttime to inquire about the miracles.

> *There was a man of the Pharisees, named Nicodemus, a ruler of the Jews: the same came to Jesus by night, and said unto him, Rabbi, we know that thou art a teacher come from God: for no man can do these miracles that thou doest, except God be with him. Jesus answered and said unto him, Verily, verily, I say unto thee, Except a man be born again, he cannot see the kingdom of God. Nicodemus saith unto him, How can a man be born when he is old? can he enter the second time into his mother's womb, and be born? Jesus answered, Verily, verily, I say unto thee, Except a man be born of water and of the Spirit, he cannot enter into the kingdom of God. That which is born of the flesh is flesh; and that which is born of the Spirit is spirit. Marvel not that I said unto thee, Ye must be born again.*
>
> —*John 3:1-7*

What was Jesus saying to this religious scholar? It was something like this: "Nicodemus, if you want to understand miracles, you must become a miracle. You must be born again." Nicodemus was about to discover that the new birth would be a greater miracle than any of the others he had heard about or even seen.

THE REASONS FOR THE NEW BIRTH

Jesus was telling Nicodemus that he needed to be radically, dramatically, and eternally changed. Why? What was wrong with Nicodemus as he was?

Born into the Natural World

Verse 4 speaks of Nicodemus's natural birth. By birth he was a descendant of Adam and therefore under the curse of sin, just like the rest of us. The apostle Paul put it this way: "[We] were by nature the children of wrath" (Ephesians 2:3). A sin nature is bred into every child born into this world. Nicodemus needed a new birth that would give him a new nature.

Bound to the Sinful World

Being a sinner by birth, Nicodemus was a sinner by practice. A man is not a sinner because he sins; he sins because he is a sinner. The real problem is the Adamic nature that comes from the first birth.

A worm hole in an apple does not mean that a worm has eaten its way into the apple. To the contrary, the worm has eaten its way out. How did the worm get inside? The egg was laid in the apple blossom. The worm was hatched in the heart of that apple.

Likewise, sin is in our hearts before it ever eats its way to the surface of our lives. Jesus made that abundantly clear:

> *But those things which proceed out of the mouth come forth from the heart; and they defile the man. For out of the heart proceed*

> *evil thoughts, murders, adulteries, fornications, thefts, false witness, blasphemies: these are the things which defile a man.*
> —*Matthew 15:18-20a*

The heart of the human problem is the problem of the human heart.

Blind to the Spiritual World

Jesus said that without the new birth, Nicodemus could not see the kingdom of God (v. 3). Nicodemus was an educated man, and yet he was blind. He had an M.I. degree ("Master of Israel," see v. 10), but he had no B.A. (Born Again) degree.

The apostle Paul describes the condition of the blindness of people without Christ when he writes that they "hav[e] the understanding darkened, being alienated from the life of God through the ignorance that is in them, because of the blindness of their heart" (Ephesians 4:18).

When a lost man says to you concerning the faith, "I just don't see it," don't scold him. He is telling the truth. He really *can't* see it.

THE REQUIREMENTS FOR THE NEW BIRTH

How does this maximum miracle of the new birth take place? For there to be a birth, there must first be a conception. Two parents are required for a child to be conceived and born in the physical realm. The same is true in the spiritual realm. The two spiritual parents for the new birth are the Spirit of God and the Word of

God. Verse 5 speaks of being born "of water and of the Spirit." "The Spirit" here is the Holy Spirit, and "water" is a symbol of the Word of God (see Ephesians 5:26).

It is the Word of God that impregnates the soul and gives new birth. The apostle Peter says we are "born again, not of corruptible seed, but of incorruptible, by the word of God, which liveth and abideth for ever" (1 Peter 1:23).

The Word of God and the Spirit of God come together in the womb of faith, and the result is a new birth, a new life in Christ. Jesus made it clear to Nicodemus that the context of this birth is faith. "For God so loved the world, that he gave his only begotten Son, that whosoever *believeth* in him should not perish, but have everlasting life" (John 3:16, emphasis added).

THE RESULTS OF THE NEW BIRTH

The maximum miracle of the new birth has some wonderful results.

A New Father

Not all people on this earth have the right to call God "Father." Only members of His forever family have that privilege. And to be in the family of God, we must be born into it. "But as many as received him, to them gave he power to become the sons of God, even to them that believe on his name" (John 1:12).

The Bible does not teach the universal Fatherhood of God and the universal brotherhood of man. Yes, we are brothers and sisters in the flesh, but spiritually we are not related until we are born from above. God is indeed the Creator of all of us, but He is only the Father of the twice-born. He is not Father by creation but by the new birth.

Because God is our Father, we have His nature within us—like Father, like son. Peter says, "Whereby are given unto us exceeding great and precious promises; that by these ye might be partakers of the divine nature, having escaped the corruption that is in the world through lust" (2 Peter 1:4).

This new nature is the birthmark of all who are born from above. There will be an inward change. If your religion has not changed your nature, you had better change your religion! Salvation is not primarily a matter of getting us out of earth and into heaven. Rather, it involves God coming into us.

What family likenesses are evident when we are made brand-new by regeneration? There will be a deep love for Christ and the Word of God. There will be an inner witness of the Holy Spirit, telling us we belong to God. There will be a desire for holiness. And there will be a desire to magnify Christ.

Another incredible blessing accompanies having a new Father. Not only do we receive His likeness—we also rest in His love. The Father loves His twice-born as much as He loves His own dear Son. This is almost too much to take in, but it is true. Listen to Jesus as He prays for His own: "I in them, and thou in me, that they may be made perfect in one; and that the world may know that thou hast sent me, and hast loved them, *as thou hast loved me*" (John 17:23, emphasis added).

Did you get that? Hallelujah! We are loved just as He is loved. The Father does not love us because we are valuable, but we are valuable because He loves us.

A New Fortune

When you are born into God's family, you are born into a very rich family. Your Father is more than able to meet your needs. "Now unto him that is able to do exceeding abundantly above all that we ask or think, according to the power that worketh in us . . . " (Ephesians 3:20). "But my God shall supply all your need according to his riches in glory by Christ Jesus" (Philippians 4:19).

We can truly sing, "My Father is rich in houses and lands. He holdeth the wealth of the world in His hands." How does it feel to be wealthy? All the King's kids are rich with heaven's treasures. You may call me "Prince Adrian."

But the best is yet to come. What we have now is just the down payment of our inheritance. We will get the full legacy of these riches in another world.

> *The Spirit itself beareth witness with our spirit, that we are the children of God: and if children, then heirs; heirs of God, and joint-heirs with Christ; if so be that we suffer with him, that we may be also glorified together. For I reckon that the sufferings of this present time are not worthy to be compared with the glory which shall be revealed in us. For the earnest expectation of the creature waiteth for the manifestation of the sons of God.*
>
> —*Romans 8:16-19*

Notice that Paul says we are "joint-heirs with Christ." Do you know what it means to be joint-heirs? It means we share and share alike. Dwell on that and it will take your breath away. Some call such anticipation "pie in the sky." Well, I like pie!

A New Future

A newborn child is all tomorrows and no yesterdays. When we come to Jesus and are born again, the past is in the grave of God's forgetfulness. We are brand-new creatures with a bright new future. And this future is absolutely secure because we are part of God's family.

But don't get the idea that it is your good behavior that keeps you in the family. I have been a Rogers all my life not because of my behavior but because I was *born* into the Rogers family.

Sometimes even my *bad* behavior reminded me I was part of the family. My dad knew how to administer corporal punishment. He would say, "Adrian, I do this because I love you." I think that I must have been his favorite!

The point is, God may chastise, but He will never disown His own dear children. Our future is not secure because of our behavior but because of our new birth. I would not trust the best fifteen minutes I ever lived to get me to heaven. So, what and whom am I trusting?

> *Unto him that is able to keep you from falling, and to present you faultless before the presence of his glory with exceeding joy, to the only wise God our Saviour, be glory and majesty, dominion and power, both now and ever. Amen.*
>
> —*Jude 24-25*

Nowhere in the Bible do we read of anyone being saved twice. Why? Because a birth happens only one time in the physical realm and only once in the spiritual realm.

THE GREAT COST

After Jesus told Nicodemus about the new birth, He mentioned that He would be lifted upon a cross. "And as Moses lifted up the serpent in the wilderness, even so must the Son of man be lifted up" (John 3:14).

Now we have some idea why the new birth is the maximum miracle. All the other miracles we have read about in this book were done easily by God's omnipotent and sovereign power. He spoke, and it came to pass. He commanded, and it was done. These miracles were no trouble at all for Him to achieve.

It did not strain Omnipotence to turn water into wine, to heal a boy near death, to restore strength to the limbs of a paralyzed man, to feed 5,000 men plus women and children with a little lad's lunch, to walk on water in the midst of a storm, to open the eyes of a man born blind, or even to raise a man from the dead. God has no trouble doing such things.

A college student asked his pastor, "Do you think there is life on other planets?" The pastor replied, "No, I really don't."

"Do you mean that in all of those billions of stars and planets in the vast universe, you don't believe there is any life?" the student asked.

"No, I really don't," the pastor repeated.

"Then tell me why God went to the trouble to make all of that."

The pastor asked, "What trouble?"

You see, and I say this with great reverence, the only time God ever had any trouble was in dark Gethsemane and at bloody Calvary. It was there that He paid for our redemption and provided for the maximum miracle, the new birth. He created universes with a word, but to save a soul He had to die in agony and blood. His soul endured hell to redeem us.

This should remind us that salvation is free, but it is not cheap. Jesus paid with the silver of His tears and the gold of His blood. This greatest miracle has cost the greatest price and brings the greatest result—eternal life.

This is why I would rather have the power to lead a soul to Christ than to raise the dead. Someone may say, "Well, Adrian, if you were really Spirit-filled, you would have the power to perform physical miracles." Not necessarily.

John the Baptist was filled with the Spirit from his mother's womb (Luke 1:15). Jesus said of John that there was not a greater person born of woman (Luke 7:28). But what was John's claim to fame? He pointed men to Jesus. He was the one who said, "Behold the Lamb of God, which taketh away the sin of the world" (John 1 :29).

One day Jesus revisited the place where John the Baptist had baptized Him. See how God records the glowing testimony concerning this Spirit-filled man and his ability to point men to Jesus: "And many resorted unto him and said, John did no miracle: but all things that John spake of this man were true. And many believed on him there" (John 10:41-42).

I say it again: I would rather have that said of me than to have the power literally to raise the dead.

GET A LIFE!

Let me sum up all I have tried to say in this book: John is interested in life—real life, eternal life. He uses the word *life* some thirty-six times in his Gospel. This life is full, abundant, and overflowing. It is a great life. Don't miss it!

A friend of mine, named Byron, is now in heaven. One time he was driving with his wife through the beautiful Smoky Mountains. His wife glanced at the dashboard and said, "Byron, we are getting low on gas. You'd better stop here at this station and fill up the tank."

But Byron said, "Don't worry about it. There will be plenty of time to get gas," and he drove on.

The Smokies were beautiful, and Byron and his wife were enjoying the drive. But his wife nodded off and went to sleep. After a while Byron noticed that the needle on the gas tank was almost at the empty mark, and there was not a gasoline station in sight!

It was now getting dark, and Byron began to think, "If I run out of gasoline on one of these dark mountain roads, we will be in serious trouble. She told me to stop and get gas. Perhaps I should have listened."

More time passed, and it seemed he was running on fumes. He was near panic. Suddenly, around a bend in the mountain road, he saw the lights of an old country store with a gasoline pump in front.

It looked so old that Byron wondered if it were an antique or if it even had gas in it. He parked the car, went inside, and asked the old mountaineer who ran the grocery store if he indeed sold gasoline. "Yep" was the reply.

Byron breathed a sigh of relief and went outside with the old man as he began to fill the tank with gasoline. It was one of those beautiful mountain evenings. Everything was working out fine.

Byron stretched out his hands, put a smile on his face, and said to the old mountaineer, "It's great to be alive, isn't it?"

The old man never even lifted his head as he replied, "I don't know. I ain't never been no other way."

Well, my friend, I have been another way! Once I was dead in trespasses and sin. But the dear Savior has come into my heart and into my life. He has given me, not mere existence, but life abundant. I can say it, even shout it: *it's great to be alive!*

Thank God for the maximum miracle of new birth and new life—eternal life—through Jesus Christ the Lord!

EPILOGUE

We have said throughout this book that God can still do the miraculous in people's lives when it serves His purpose and brings Him glory. His mighty hand is not shortened in these days!

With that in mind, we want to close this book with several testimonies of modern-day miracles—works of glory and grace that God has performed in the lives of the believers you will meet in the following pages. In each case God was glorified. Each miracle is well documented, and we have the permission of the people involved to share these stories (most told in their own words).

I trust you will be blessed and encouraged by these testimonies to God's miraculous, compassionate power.

A BELOVED WIFE RESTORED

by R. Kent Hughes[1]

Do we really need the Saviour? Do we really need a "Wonderful Counselor, Mighty God, Everlasting Father, Prince of Peace"?

Will you let me share a personal story with you? Though I would rather not focus on my own experience, nevertheless there are times when God does such a work in one's life that it is a sin to remain silent. And although what I have to share is in the first person, it really is a story about God. May all the glory go to His name!

It was only supposed to be routine surgery, but something went wrong. And the life of my beloved wife, Barbara, hung in the balance by the thinnest thread.

Early in the morning I had checked Barbara into the hospital and settled back to wait. As I was reading the morning paper, I recognized a medical technician named Suzanne and cheerfully greeted her. Suzanne had become friends with my wife's niece when they both had worked in the hospital some years before.

Barbara's niece had long since moved away, and it was quite unexpected to run into Suzanne—especially since she normally didn't come to the waiting room area where I was sitting that morning.

My oldest daughter, Holly, joined me, and at 10 A.M. the surgeon met with us and cheerfully announced that everything was "perfect, it couldn't have gone better." Barbara would be in the recovery room for an hour and a half, and then I could see her. So Holly and I agreed that I would go home, do a few chores, and we'd see Barbara together a little later.

But when I returned, I was met by my worried daughter who informed me that they had taken Barbara back into surgery. It was only supposed to take fifteen minutes, but those fifteen minutes stretched to five hours. We soon realized something was seriously wrong. They couldn't stop the bleeding, and no one on the team of doctors could figure out why. The day stretched into the evening without any answer.

Thus began a very long, dark night. Barbara sensed her life was slipping away. After her doctor's visit at 11 P.M. matters only worsened. Nurses repeatedly changed the dressing, but Barbara continued to hemorrhage and kept growing weaker. At 1:30 I called our associate pastor to start a prayer vigil, and I got more than I'd asked for as all the staff and several friends arrived within the hour to pray.

By the middle of the next day, however, it looked as if I was going to lose my beloved wife. By then she had lost two-thirds of her body's blood. Her heart was racing, and she kept bleeding. As family members gathered around the bed, Larry Fullerton, my associate pastor, commented, "You need to encourage her. She thinks she's going to die. Her blood isn't clotting."

Remember Suzanne? She had seen me the previous morning and now happened to stop by at just that moment to say hi and give Barbara some magazines. Shocked to walk in on a family crisis, she felt like she really shouldn't be there, but stayed long enough to hear Larry's comment about "her blood not clotting."

In that instant Suzanne remembered doing a blood test years ago on Barbara's niece. When she had showed the results to a blood specialist, the niece was warned that if she were ever in a car accident or suffered a similar trauma she could bleed to death. Suzanne ran to the lab, switched on her computer, called up the niece's records, and compared them with Barbara's workup: the pathology was identical!

Suzanne then ran to the critical care unit and tried to explain all this to the nurse. She then dashed back to her supervisor, who told her to go immediately to the blood bank. As Suzanne began to explain, the blood bank doctor exclaimed, "Barbara Hughes! Tell Dr. _____!" Barging into the doctor's meeting with five pathologists, Suzanne told her story. Within the hour Barbara was given the medication for her rare blood disorder—and her life was saved.

But this is not a story about Barbara or Suzanne. It is a story about God. What happened to my wife and Suzanne is a miracle of divine providence. There is no other way to explain it. It really started years ago—when two bored lab technicians ran tests on each other, and one (Suzanne) learned that the other (who happened to be my wife's niece) had a rare clotting disorder. Then on the day of Barbara's surgery, I ran into this lab technician—who normally doesn't come to the area where I was—and mentioned Barbara's surgery. The next day Suzanne stopped by to see Barbara at exactly the right moment to overhear Larry's comment. Amazingly Suzanne remembered those tests from years ago.

Suzanne saved my wife's life. But was it really Suzanne who saved Barbara? No. God did! It was God in His sovereign care who orchestrated the miraculous details of these events.

TIM'S MIRACLE
Told by Jan Barger

The day my son Timothy Barger lost his memory started out like any other Montrose day in July, although it was unusually hot for this little town snuggled in the foothills of the Endless Mountains of Pennsylvania.

It was the next-to-the-last day of camp for Tim and his three cousins at the Montrose Bible Conference, founded in 1908 by his great-great-grandfather, Reuben A. Torrey. The campers were outside playing a game of "capture the flag." Tim's asthma was beginning to act up, so he went to see the nurse. She gave him his Ventolin, and he hyperventilated a bit. After using the rebreathing bag, Tim said he felt better and was going to go back outside. Just then, the camp nurse said, Tim's eyes glazed over. He didn't know where he was, who she was, or who he was.

That's how it began. Tim's memory was suddenly and completely gone. It was as though all eleven years of his life had been wiped from his mind's computer. He didn't know his grandmother or his cousins; he didn't recognize me (his mother) or his sister. He had to be retaught how to brush his teeth, take a shower, and talk on the phone.

Tim didn't remember anything about his life. But he could ride his bike, swim, tie his shoes, play computer games and chess, do math, spell, read and write at grade level. Back home, Tim said, "Mommy, this is like being in a whole new town. I don't know anyone or anything." Trying to explain what had happened to him when we didn't understand it ourselves was difficult at best. Many of his friends thought he was just fooling, although for the most part they were very helpful.

After meeting with his teachers, we went ahead and put him into his regular sixth grade class in middle school, trusting God that Tim would be able to cope. He had panic attacks around large groups of people, and when he got upset he would start vomiting, which happened three or four times a day.

Then a new wrinkle emerged. Whenever Tim's body temperature rose above 99 degrees, he would get dizzy and show signs of heat exhaustion, pass out, and be unable to move his extremities, sit up, swallow, or even talk until his body temperature cooled. I would race over to the school as soon as it happened and stay with him for fifteen to twenty minutes until he came to and was able to walk and talk again; then he would go back to class.

Because of the large numbers of people present, each time we tried to take Timothy to church he would have a panic attack. Our prayer was that Tim would be able to make it through a service by Christmas Eve so we could attend as a family. God graciously answered that prayer, and by the first of the year we were in church together again.

Tim's physicians were completely puzzled. We made the rounds from pediatric neurologists (the first one told us his memory would return in two weeks) to psychiatrists, psychologists, pediatricians, an endocrinologist, and back to neurologists. He had a CAT scan, MRIs, MRA, EEGs, and a myriad of blood tests—all normal.

Tim had two batteries of psychological and psychiatric testing, and even one session of hypnosis, but nothing showed up. We were quite certain he had suffered some type of stroke, something so unusual that it didn't show up on an MRI or CAT scan. Though none of the doctors would give any credence to our theory, none of them had any logical explanation.

Nor, to our great surprise, were any of them interested in pursuing Tim's case. He certainly was unusual, they admitted, but once his tests came back normal, they wanted no more involvement. From a medical perspective my husband, Bob, and I were on our own.

Throughout this time we were surrounded by the love and

prayers of our church family and of believers literally around the world. Not a day went by that a member of our family did not receive some expression of love or concern. That September the elders of the church prayed for and anointed Tim with oil, according to James 5. To see these wonderful men of God surrounding our little boy, blanketing him with prayer, and to witness their tears along with ours was a powerful blessing. Bob and I experienced healing in our own souls that day.

God gave us a special friend during this time, a psychiatrist who was new to our church and had just started attending our Sunday school class. He was the one who believed Tim had had a stroke, and he believed Tim could be healed. He and his lovely wife (a dermatologist) gave us some very practical suggestions about how to cope with Tim's heat exhaustion.

My youngest sister, Lyn Newbrander, a missionary in Berlin, E-mailed us fairly regularly. At one point I mentioned that Tim had stopped vomiting at school, sometime in October. "Oh!" she cried. "That's just when the children and I decided we were going to pray for something specific for Tim, and we decided that we would pray that he would stop vomiting!"

God does answer prayer. I had evidence of it. But still . . . Another time, as I was questioning God's goodness and wondering why He wanted Tim to go through this, Lyn wrote back, saying she didn't think God wanted Tim to go through this and that she was praying for his complete and total healing. "I know that you and Bobby are willing to do anything for Tim's complete recovery, and I want you to know that I'm willing to do whatever God wants me to do too."

That struck a chord with me. No more wimpy prayers for bits

and pieces of healing or finding the right physician or test, but rather total and complete dependence on God. I shared Lyn's letter and our resolve with my Sunday school class, who had been praying faithfully with us.

By now Tim was able to make it through Sunday school if the room wasn't too hot. He would take an insulated bottle of ice and water and a small battery-operated fan to keep cool. He could get through school and church most days without an episode. School was going well, and his grades were good.

The weather was cold and rather miserable throughout that spring. Every day Bob and I would thank the Lord for temperatures below 68 degrees. Another day made just for Tim!

Several weeks later, we were all in church together. Bob was ushering. During the congregational prayer Tim tugged at my sleeve. "Mommy, I remember something," he whispered. "I remember Jill's [his sister's] fourteenth birthday. We had donuts and went to Buttermilk Falls!" His hands were icy cold, and he started to cry. We stumbled out of the pew and into the narthex.

"Honey, what else do you remember?" I asked him. "Do you remember going to Disney World?"

"Yes, and we went to Epcot Center where they have all those little villages." The memories began to tumble out. Everything seemed to be there, from the memories of the old carpet in the living room, to the day that he asked Jesus into his heart, to silly times with his sisters, to camp in Montrose, to songs that he knew.

We laughed, cried, and praised God. After nine and a half long months, it was as though a closed door in his mind had suddenly opened, and everything stored up there was released.

The following week we must have asked Tim a dozen times

to tell us a memory. His delight in suddenly knowing his friends in a more complete way was a joy to behold. His sense of humor began to bubble forth. He began to whistle and sing around the house, and he could once again say "Good morning" in German.

He had three more heat exhaustion episodes that week, including one during an EEG when we had him exercise with a sweatshirt on in a hot room to see if we could capture his reaction on video. He passed out, but later the neurologist called us to say that despite seeing what happened to him on the video, there was nothing that showed up in Tim's brain waves. They were completely normal.

I believe they were normal because that was Tim's last episode. God had healed him of the heat exhaustion too.

Some time later we received another E-mail from Lyn. "I've been wondering why God chose to heal Tim in this way. And early this morning when I couldn't sleep, I was prompted to look at Isaiah 42:8. It says, 'I am the Lord; that is my name! I will not give my glory to another.' I think God chose to heal Tim in this manner so that NO ONE could take the credit except God! He certainly wasn't on any medication, nor was he in therapy, or being treated by a physician. He wasn't even being prayed for by a specific person at that time, so no one can even claim it was their prayer that did it. No, only God can take the glory for his healing!"

A few days after that, I was reading Psalms for my devotions and came across Psalm 63:2: "I have seen you in the sanctuary and beheld your power and your glory."

"Lord," I exulted, "I've not only seen You in the sanctuary, I can point to the pew! "

God not only watches over us with tender, loving care—He

pays attention to detail. You see, the day Tim's memory was restored was Mother's Day!

AN HONEST DOUBTER

One more time I, Adrian Rogers, want to emphasize that *the greatest miracle is the miracle of God's redeeming grace.* Let me tell one final story that illustrates how the Gospel of John can help us discover this glorious truth.

He came into my office. He was brusque and straightforward. He said, "Mr. Rogers, I need to speak with you. My wife wants to commit suicide, and I don't want her to. Would you talk with her?"

I had never met the man before. I found out that he was high up in the space industry. He had a well-paying job and was part of the intelligentsia that helped America put a man on the moon in the late 1960s.

I told him that I would speak with his wife if he would come with her. We had not been in counseling very long before I discovered that he was her problem. This man had abused his wife in many ways. He was given to alcohol, gambling, adultery, and physical and verbal abuse.

I stopped talking to her and fastened my eyes upon him. "Are you a Christian?" I asked him. Understand that I was not asking for information but only to get the conversation started.

He scornfully laughed and said, "No, I am not a Christian. I am an atheist." I said, "Indeed. You know there is no God?" He said, "That's right."

I said, "May I then ask you a question? Do you know all there is to know?" "Of course not," he said. I said, "Would it be generous to say that you know half of all there is to know?" "Very generous," he answered. I said, "All right then, how do you know that God does not exist in the other half of the knowledge that you do not know?"

He said, "Okay, then I am not an atheist. I am an agnostic." I said, "Now we are getting somewhere." I didn't tell him that the Latin equivalent for *agnostic* is ignoramus. I said to him, "Well, an agnostic is a doubter. You don't know there is a God, you just doubt that there is one." He said, "Yes, I am a doubter—a big one."

I said to him, "I don't care what size, I just want to know what kind. There are two kinds—honest doubters and dishonest doubters. What kind are you?"

He said, "What's the difference?" I said, "The difference is this—an honest doubter doesn't know but because he is honest he wants to know, and therefore he makes an honest investigation. A dishonest doubter doesn't know because he doesn't want to know. He can't find God for the same reason a thief can't find a policeman."

This man said to me, "Well, I would like to think that I am honest." I said, "Wonderful. How would you like to put God in the laboratory and prove whether or not He exists?" He said, "It can't be done." I said, "It can be done if you get in the right laboratory. Let me give you a challenge that Jesus made."

I then quoted to him this verse from the Gospel of John: "If any man will do his will, he shall know of the doctrine, whether it be of God, or whether I speak of myself" (John 7:17).

I told him in plain English that verse means that if a man

desires to do the will of God, God will reveal Himself to that man. He said, "How does it work?"

I said, "Would you be willing to sign a statement like this? 'God, I don't know whether You exist or not, I don't know whether Jesus is Your Son or not, I don't know whether the Bible is Your Word or not; but I want to know. And because I want to know, I will make an honest investigation, and because it is an honest investigation, I will follow the results of that investigation wherever they lead me regardless of the cost.'" He said, "Give it to me again." I repeated it. He said, "Yes, I would be willing to sign that." I said, "Wonderful! Now here is what I want to suggest to you. There is one book of the Bible, the Gospel of John, that was written so that you might believe that Jesus is the Christ and so that by believing you might have eternal life.

"I want to give you this challenge—begin to read the Gospel of John and say something like this, but say it honestly: 'God, if You exist, if this is Your Word, if it is true, reveal it to me; and I will follow it wherever it leads me. If You don't convince me that it is true, I will continue the same way that I am.'" I admonished him, however, to make certain that he was absolutely honest that he would obey the truth if God revealed it to him.

True to his word, he began to read the Gospel of John with his will surrendered at the front end to whatever truth might come. Weeks later he came by my office, got on his knees, and with tears gave his heart to Jesus Christ and was transformed.

The last time I saw that man and his wife, they were sitting in their white Cadillac, holding hands like school kids. She had given her heart to Christ. They were both in love with Jesus and in love with one another.

That was over twenty-five years ago. I lost track of this man until I recently received a letter from him. He is now living in the state of Maine. He is active in his church and is actually helping get out the Gospel through Christian tapes and is serving on the board of a Christian school. He told me what God is doing in his life, and then he said something I think I shall never forget. He said, "Mr. Rogers, thank you for spending time with this general in the Devil's army."

Again, that is the great miracle. The Gospel of John, read with an open heart and a surrendered will, will lead one to this conclusion—that Jesus is the Christ, the Son of the living God, and beyond that to a saving faith. This is the great miracle.

NOTES

CHAPTER 1:
THE POSSIBILITY OF MIRACLES

1. Marolyn Ford with Phyllis Boykin, *These Blind Eyes Now See* (Wheaton, Ill.: Victor Books, 1977), pp. 113-116.
2. Justice Scalia, *Intercessors for America Newsletter*, Vol. 28, No. 6, June 1996, p. 3.

CHAPTER 2:
THE PROBLEMS WITH MIRACLES

1. Peter Wagner, *The Baptist Message*, January 18, 1996, p. 7.
2. Thomas Wang, ibid, p. 6.
3. Jerry Rankin, ibid.

CHAPTER 3:
WATER INTO WINE

1. Adapted from "Dr. Dobson Answers Your Questions," *Focus on the Family*, August 1996, p. 5.

CHAPTER 8:
OPENING BLIND EYES

1. Robert J. Krigel, *If It Ain't Broke, Break It* (New York: Warner Books, 1991), flyleaf.

EPILOGUE

1. R. Kent Hughes, *The Saviour* (Wheaton, Ill.: Crossway Books, 1995), pp. 5-7.

Dr. Adrian Rogers, founder and president of Love Worth Finding Ministries is heard over syndicated radio, television, and cable systems throughout North America and many parts of the world. For broadcast and other information, call 1-800-274-5683 or write:

Love Worth Finding Ministries
Box 38-300
Memphis, Tennessee 38183